Contents

Preface and Acknowledgments   vii
List of Tables   ix
List of Abbreviations   xi

Chapter 1   Introduction   1
Chapter 2   Gender, Work and Union Activism   11
Chapter 3   Background to the Study   35
Chapter 4   Shop Steward Activism and Occupational
              Position   53
Chapter 5   Gender and Union Office-Holding   84
Chapter 6   Gender, Collective Bargaining and Union
              Policy Issues   128
Chapter 7   Conclusion   151

Bibliography   157
Index   167

To the trade union activists of Sheffield UNISON 2 Branch (formerly Sheffield NALGO) who participated in the research which made this book possible.

Preface and Acknowledgments

This book developed out of my academic and political interests in women's position in trade unions. As a lecturer in higher education, I have taught Industrial Sociology and Women's Studies for many years. I have also as a trade unionist been involved personally in the process of feminization of trade unions described in this book. I have served on Trades Councils and their Women's Sub-committees in Newcastle and Sheffield. I have been, and am, an active member of NATFHE (National Association of Teachers in Further and Higher Education), holding office as a local negotiator and regional and national delegate. This book is written from the perspective that in the last two decades feminists have achieved a substantial improvement in the level of trade union support for women's rights, although there is still much to be done to advance the position of women workers, both within employment and within trade unions.

I would like to acknowledge the support of a number of friends and colleagues who have contributed to the completion of this research. These include Eileen Green, Dr Diana Woodward and Dr John Gill (supervisors of my PhD thesis), Dr Kate Purcell and Professor Kenneth Roberts (examiners of my PhD thesis), Dr Harriet Bradley for her helpful advice in the writing of this book, and academic colleagues who have shared my interest in women and trade unions and discussed the work with me at particular stages of its development, including Dr Theresa Rees and Dr Frieda Rozen.

Above all I would like to thank the shop stewards and union officers who, despite the demands of their work and trade union activity, gave up their time to answer questionnaires and be interviewed for the research. This book attempts to tell part of their story, in terms of the growing awareness and support of trade unions for women's rights, and the survival and achievements of trade unions in difficult times.

Elizabeth Lawrence
October 1993

List of Tables

Table 4.1	Classification of Departments by Gender	57
Table 4.2	Informants Answering Questionnaire, by Occupational Status	64
Table 4.3	Shop Stewards' Views of NALGO's Negotiating Priorities	69
Table 4.4	Experiences of Industrial Action as a Member of NALGO — All Shop Stewards	71
Table 4.5	Hours per Week Spent on NALGO Work — All Shop Stewards	75
Table 4.6	Sources of Difficulty in Taking Time Off for Union Work — All Shop Stewards	76
Table 4.7	Times when Union Work Performed, by Occupational Status	78
Table 4.8	Job Support for Union Work — All Shop Stewards	79
Table 4.9	Job Conflicts with Union Work — All Shop Stewards	79
Table 4.10	Access to Information from Job Useful for Union Work	79
Table 4.11	Conflict of Time Demands between Job and Union Work	80
Table 5.1	Shop Stewards Answering the Questionnaire, by Occupational Status and Gender	86
Table 5.2	Interviewees by Occupational Status and Gender	86
Table 5.3	Annual Numbers of Male and Female Shop Stewards in the Sheffield NALGO Local Government Branch	87
Table 5.4	Presence of Children among Shop Stewards, by Gender of Shop Steward	88
Table 5.5	Age of Youngest Child of Shop Stewards, by Gender of Shop Steward	88

List of Tables

Table 5.6   Shop Stewards Asked to Stand for Election by Work Colleagues   95

Table 5.7   Experience of Industrial Action as a Member of NALGO — Male and Female Shop Stewards   103

Table 5.8   Hours per Week Spent on NALGO Work, by Gender   106

Table 5.9   Times when Union Work Performed, by Gender   106

Table 5.10   Difficulties in Taking Time Off for Union Work, by Gender   107

Table 5.11   Sources of Difficulty in Taking Time Off for Union Work, by Gender   107

Table 5.12   Job Support for Union Work, by Gender   108

Table 5.13   Job Conflicts with Union Work, by Gender   108

Table 6.1   Views of NALGO's Negotiating Priorities — Male Shop Stewards   130

Table 6.2   Views of NALGO's Negotiating Priorities — Female Shop Stewards   131

Table 6.3   Shop Stewards' Views of Gender Inequality in Society   141

List of Abbreviations

ACTT	Association of Cinematograph, Television and Allied Technicians
AEU	Amalgamated Engineering Union
AFL	American Federation of Labor
APEX	Association of Professional, Executive, Clerical, and Computer Staff
APT&C	Administrative, Professional, Technical and Clerical
ASTMS	Association of Scientific, Technical and Managerial Staffs
CLUW	Coalition of Labor Union Women
CND	Campaign for Nuclear Disarmament
COHSE	Confederation of Health Service Employees
DLP	District Labour Party
F&CS	Family and Community Services
GMB	GMB Union [previously General, Municipal, Boilermakers and Allied Trades Union]
GMWU	General and Municipal Workers' Union
HERE	Hotel Employees and Restaurant Employees
ICFTU	International Confederation of Free Trade Unions
LRD	Labour Research Department
MATSA	Managerial, Administrative, Technical and Supervisory Association
NAC	National Abortion Campaign
NALGO	National and Local Government Officers' Association
NATFHE	National Association of Teachers in Further and Higher Education
NEC	National Executive Committee
NUPE	National Union of Public Employees
NUT	National Union of Teachers
PO	Principal Officer
SEIU	Service Employees' International Union
SERTUC	South East Regional Council of the TUC

SO	Senior Officer
SOGAT	Society of Graphical and Allied Trades
TUC	Trades Union Congress
Union WAGE	Union Women's Alliance to Gain Equality
USDAW	Union of Shop, Distributive and Allied Workers

Chapter 1

Introduction

Women workers are now a third of trade union members in Britain (LRD, 1991). During the 1970s and 1980s there were a number of major developments in trade union policies on women's rights. More women came through to positions of trade union leadership, although women are still under-represented in many areas. Women and issues of women's rights moved to a more central position, if not yet exactly centre stage, in the labour movement.

This 'feminizing' of the labour movement built upon decades of work by women trade unionists such as Emma Paterson, who founded and led the Women's Trade Union League from 1874 to 1886, and Mary Macarthur, who led the National Federation of Women Workers from 1906 to 1920. The progress that women have made within the trade union movement is one of the quiet success stories of feminism. In 1988 at the TUC Conference, Norman Willis, General Secretary of the TUC, spoke of the labour movement as a movement which had been received from our forefathers and would be handed down to our daughters and granddaughters.

This study narrates one small part of this general picture. It is a study of male and female shop stewards in Sheffield NALGO (National and Local Government Officers' Association) and explores issues of gender and union activism in this context. NALGO has now merged with COHSE (Confederation of Health Service Employees) and NUPE (National Union of Public Employees) to form UNISON, a public sector union with 1.4 million members, over two-thirds of whom are women.

The Continuing Relevance of Trade Unions

While trade unions may have become unfashionable in Britain in the 1980s, they are still important institutions of civil society, as the emergence of independent trade unions in the former Soviet Union and Eastern Europe illustrates. In Britain TUC-affiliated unions still have over seven million members. Around a quarter (26 per cent) of Britain's eleven million women workers are members of trade unions. Despite the failings at times of trade unions to represent female members' interests adequately in collective bargaining, women workers are still generally better off in terms of pay and conditions of service if they work in unionized employment (Martin and Roberts, 1984).

Women's position in trade unions has been and still is important in respect of women's position in society generally. For many working-class people trade unions were a route to public office-holding, as councillors, members of parliament, magistrates, and representatives on many public bodies. The Hansard report 'Women at the Top' (1990) includes unions as an important sector of public life. Union activism can develop women's leadership skills in society generally. There are around 2.7 million women trade union members in Britain today (LRD, 1991), far more than there are women managers (Hansard, 1990). Nonetheless, trade union women have been a much less favoured group for academic research in recent years than women managers.

Trade unions have an important role to play in promoting women's equality in employment. Unions have campaigned and negotiated for the development of equal opportunities programmes in the workplace (Ellis, 1981, 1988; TUC, 1986). As collective organizations, they can also set examples of good practice within the workplace in terms of representation of women members, which can influence the general organizational culture. Hence the development of union policies on women's rights, and equality for women within trade unions, is important for the success of equal opportunities policies in employment generally.

Women in Trade Unions

There is a relative lack of research into women's present-day situation in the unions. Far more historical than contemporary studies have been conducted. It is appropriate to indicate very briefly here some of the lessons from women's trade union history to show how they illuminate women's position in unions today. One of the first obvious features of women's trade union history is the instances of women's exclusion from male-dominated unions. For example the engineering union in Britain, the AEU (Amalgamated Engineering Union) did not admit women into membership until 1943. Many unions, along with employers and Victorian social reformers, sought to restrict women's role in paid employment, so that women would be confined to an exclusively domestic role. They thus espoused the ideology of the family wage, which undermined the claims of women workers to equal pay. Women workers in the nineteenth and twentieth centuries have therefore been obliged to wage long battles for their right to work in paid employment.

The struggle for equal pay has been equally lengthy. The TUC passed a resolution in support of equal pay in 1888, but there was little progress for many decades after that. In the 1950s equal pay was achieved by trade union negotiation in the civil service, local government and teaching. The 1968 equal pay strike by Ford's machinists at Dagenham achieved the 1970 Equal Pay Act. This led to a wave of equal pay strikes, such as that at Trico-Folberth, and industrial tribunal applications. European law produced the 1984 Equal Pay Amendment Act, which brought in the equal value regulations. It was under the wider definition of equal pay, as equal pay for work of equal value, introduced by the 1984 Act, that the Ford's machinists finally achieved the regrading they had originally sought in 1968, following a further equal pay strike in 1986. Nonetheless, despite these achievements, women workers still receive far from equal pay. In 1992 women's average gross hourly earnings were 78.8 per cent of men's (LRD, 1993).

Women workers have also had to fight for their rightful place within the trade union movement. In the nineteenth century women workers were obliged to form single-sex unions in many trades because male workers would not admit women to their unions. The major exceptions to this pattern were the textile unions. Thus, in the past, single-sex unionism for women did not represent any feminist principle of separatism, but rather a necessary detour on the path to union organization which was forced on women workers.

While there have been a few attempts to set up women-only unions, most women trade unionists in the twentieth century have not sought separate organization. They have campaigned within unions for the establishment of advisory committees and conferences on women's rights, and for reserved places on leadership bodies for women. Not all women trade unionists have supported these measures, since some have argued that reserved places are patronizing and tokenist and that special women's conferences and committees can ghettoize women and women's issues. The majority of feminists active within unions, however, have seen these measures as useful for giving a focus to women's concerns and providing support for women who wish to take up these issues.

Within the unions women have made progress but in many

unions they are still under-represented in positions of leadership. A
Labour Research Department Survey found that in 1990 women were
34 per cent of the membership of TUC-affiliated unions, but were
only 20 per cent of national executive committee members, 23 per
cent of delegates to union conferences, 21 per cent of TUC delega-
tions and 20 per cent of national full-time officials of unions (LRD,
1991). While these figures, and the very fact that many trade unions
now keep records of levels of female representation, show some improvement from much greater levels of under-representation in the
past, there is still a considerable way to go for women to be represented in positions of union leadership commensurate with their
numbers in the unions. There is a need for far more research to
document how women's position in the unions is changing and to
show what changes are needed for the future.

Trade union activism presents feminists with the issue of working
alongside men. This is not only because the majority of trade unionists
are male. It also arises from the essential nature of trade unions as
collective organizations, whose strength lies in their inclusiveness and
their ability to recruit all the workers in the field they are organizing.
Activists within trade unions therefore are generally committed to the
principle of worker unity. It would be difficult to be active within
trade unions for a long time and to regard men as the main enemy.

Trade unions are one area where the feminist agenda has been
far more concerned with emphasizing solidarity between women and
men and the similarities between male and female workers rather
than the differences. This is clear in respect of central feminist issues
in relation to employment, such as equal pay, equal job opportunity
and access to training. Claims for equal treatment in these areas rest
essentially upon the argument that both sexes are capable of doing the
same work. There have, however, been other areas where issues of
difference have necessarily been addressed, such as sexual harassment,
abortion rights and maternity/paternity leave. Nonetheless even here
the debate within the trade unions has often focused on the need to
address these issues so that women can be equal within the world of
paid work. Much trade union feminism thus rests upon liberal and
socialist feminist traditions which see the differences between men
and women as minimal, limited to reproductive role, and not properly
relevant to the workplace.

It is, however, increasingly recognized within trade unions that
the unity of a trade union must be built on the basis of both emphasizing solidarity and respecting diversity. Thus there has been a growing
acceptance of the usefulness of specialist committees and conferences

4

for particular groups, such as female, black, gay and disabled members. There is also an on-going debate within trade unions about the extent to which male and female workers have the same or different priorities for collective bargaining and union organizing.

Women's under-representation in union leadership is an issue which was debated in many sections of the trade union movement in the 1980s. This followed the adoption by many unions in the 1970s of policies on women's rights and the establishment or re-activation of women's rights or equal rights committees. There was an increasing recognition by trade unionists of the necessity for adequate representation of women in union office-holding if policies on women's rights were to become effective. This encouraged several unions, including NALGO, to conduct surveys of women's representation and levels of office-holding and to seek to promote women's participation (Rees and Reed, 1981).

The Impact of Gender and Work on Union Activism

Given that the focus of this book is gender and trade unions, rather than the much wider field of gender and employment, this account does not deal at length with gender inequalities in employment which are competently documented and analyzed in many studies (Charles, 1993; Rees, 1992). Nonetheless, in order to explain where occupational differences and inequalities are relevant to the explanation of gender differences within the unions, a few general remarks about the relation between gender roles and work roles are appropriate.

Gender roles and work roles are interrelated in a number of ways. Gender roles influence position in the occupational structure. Occupational segregation by sex is a major feature of employment and has been explained by a variety of economic and sociological theories. The influence, however, is not purely one-way from gender role to occupational position. It is not just that the gender role in society determines experience in the workplace. Occupational experience can alter women's and men's understanding and performance of their gender roles, as can union activism. Thus greater equality in the workplace can contribute substantially to changing women's position in society as a whole.

Feldberg and Glenn (1979) argue that too often in industrial sociology women's work experience has been studied through the perspective of a gender model, so that attitudes to work and to career progression are all explained in terms of family position and the

female model [handwritten]

Interview 5 [handwritten]

feminine gender role. Meanwhile men's work experience has been studied through the perspective of a work model, in which attitudes and behaviour at work are all explained in terms of the nature of work, neglecting the possible influence of family and the masculine gender role. They argue that what is needed is 'an integrated model which takes into account the interaction between job and gender factors' (p. 527). This argument can be applied also to the study of trade union activism. It is important for feminists to take women's work experiences seriously and avoid the tendency to explain all gender differences in employment as a result of family role or gender socialization, since this ignores inequalities arising from the workplace.

In studying gender differences at work, it is important to be clear whether the focus of study is gender differences arising from gender roles in society or differences at work which occur along gender lines. In short, are the differences really gender differences or occupational differences? Are they differences which arise because men and women have experienced different socialization or differences which arise because men and women work in different jobs? This is an important theoretical question in Women's Studies and in the sociology of gender. Often when social scientists speak of a gender difference, the same term is employed to cover both meanings. This can lead to confusion. Because a difference occurs along gender lines, it does not automatically follow that it is the direct result of gender roles.

An example from the case of union organization among part-time workers illustrates this distinction. Fryer *et al.* (1978) in their work on facilities for shop stewards in NUPE (National Union of Public Employees) found that the main obstacle facing many women members of the union in becoming a shop steward was that they worked part-time, which made it difficult to be in full-time contact with the members they would represent as a shop steward. Thus the factor inhibiting union involvement was being a part-time worker (an occupational factor) rather than being a woman (a gender role factor). This example shows the need for rigorous and careful thinking about whether differences between women's and men's work situation and union involvement should be explained in terms of occupational or gender role factors. An awareness of the importance of occupation can also help in understanding differences among women in terms of attitudes to work and involvement in unions.

Any workable model of union participation has to examine both those factors which motivate and enable members to participate and hold office in unions and also obstacles and disincentives to participation. This is particularly so in the case of women workers, given the past failures of some unions to provide women with positive reasons for participating. It is, for instance, inaccurate to assume that, if women were freed of childcare or other domestic responsibilities, the extra time available would necessarily lead to increased levels of union activism. While the significance of such barriers should not be underestimated, women's union participation cannot be explained only in terms of obstacles to participation arising from women's gender role; factors such as occupational role and work situation also need to be taken into account.

Moreover, it should not be assumed that the feminine gender role is always a demotivating factor in terms of union activism. While certain forms of union militancy may ostensibly conflict with traditional forms of femininity, for some informants in the research reported in this book, such as the nursery nurses who became shop stewards, it was precisely the contradictions of the feminine gender role which were one of the motivating forces for union activism. Conversely, the masculine gender role sometimes assisted male shop stewards to be promoted in the workplace and hence removed from union office-holding. It is too often ignored in industrial sociology literature that male workers have gender roles, which may influence many aspects of work behaviour including union activism. This study attempts to contribute to remedying this imbalance by giving proper attention to men's gender roles and women's occupational roles.

The Study of Sheffield NALGO

The research is based upon a study of shop stewards and lay union officers in the Sheffield Local Government Branch of NALGO. The research on Sheffield NALGO was designed to explore the relationship between gender, work and union activism. The form of union activism examined in this study is office-holding, either at shop steward or branch officer level. This reflected the parliamentary structure of NALGO, where membership constituencies sent their shop steward to the branch executive. The focus on union office-holding is not intended to downplay the importance of other forms of union activism, particularly membership participation. Nonetheless the issue of union office-holding merits study in order to measure and understand women's representation in trade unions. This book does identify patterns of female under-representation in union office-holding. It also explores the way male and female shop stewards and lay union officers balanced their work, home and union lives. It is hoped that this study will be of interest to both union activists and academic researchers who are committed to increasing women's levels of representation in trade unions and making trade unions more woman-friendly.

The fieldwork, carried out between 1987 and 1990, involved a questionnaire study of the shop steward population, interviews with twenty-four branch officers and shop stewards and a study of the branch records of shop stewards from 1983 to 1989. In the Sheffield NALGO Local Government Branch the membership was split approximately 50/50 between men and women, but about two-thirds of the shop stewards were men. Sixty-four shop stewards replied to the question-naire, forty-two men and twenty-two women. The branch offered an opportunity to investigate the widely occuring phenomenon of under-representation of women in union office-holding. It was also an oppor-tunity to explore issues of gender equality in a union branch where many activists possessed a strong commitment to equal opportunities.

The Sheffield NALGO Local Government Branch was chosen for the research project because it offered the opportunity to study a sizeable population of union office-holders of both sexes at a range of levels in the occupational hierarchy and in a variety of different depart-ments. It thus offered an ideal opportunity for investigating the influ-ence of occupation, gender and department on union office-holding. As the material discussed in Chapter 3 regarding the history and environment of the branch shows, it also provided substantial material for sociological analysis, situated as it was in a Labour-controlled city where the influence of unions based in heavy industry, such as engi-neering and steel, had played an important role in the history of the local labour movement. The branch had also recently been involved in major local and national disputes as well as facing many industrial and political problems relating to local government finance and the issues of rate-capping and the poll tax.

There were two existing research studies which provided impor-tant coordinates for the research. The study by Nicholson, Ursell and Blyton (1981) of the Sheffield NALGO Local Government Branch provided much valuable material about the recent history of the branch, including the introduction of the shop steward system, and explored at length the relation between grade and union office-holding. It identified the under-representation of women in low-grade jobs in union office-holding, but did not explore fully the dimensions of gender inequality. The study by Stone (1984) of women's position in Council employ-ment not only documented the existing gender inequalities, but revealed their departmental distribution, with more higher-grade posts being located in the predominantly male departments.

Structure of the Book

This introductory chapter outlines the main themes of the book, namely
the influences of work and gender on union activism. Chapter 2 provides
a literature review of women's position in trade unions and theories of
union participation, together with a discussion of how women's position
in trade unions changed during the 1970s and 1980s. It thus situates
the research in relation to other academic studies and the changing
position of women in trade unions.

Chapter 3 sets the research in its national and local (Sheffield)
contexts, giving a brief history of the branch, a short discussion of the
Sheffield context, and a summary of relevant aspects of NALGO,
including NALGO's first national strike of 1989.

The main reporting of the research findings is contained in Chapters 4, 5 and 6. Chapter 4 discusses the material concerning occupational position, starting with an account of the occupational structure
in local government and NALGO's involvement in its creation and re-
negotiation. The understanding of this structure is important for the
study of how occupational segregation by sex occurs in local government and influences patterns of union office-holding. The second
part of Chapter 4 discusses the relationship between occupation and
job grade and union office-holding. This consideration of occupational
differences is important to identify the extent to which differences
between men and women were differences arising from gender role or
from employment in different jobs.

Chapter 4 also contains some discussion of differences in organizational cultures according to the department individuals worked in.
Different departments tended to have different cultures and histories
of union organization. It is important to consider this as an aspect of
the influence of work on union activism, particularly because departmental cultures usually have a definite gender dimension. For instance
female leadership was much more acceptable in the Departments of
Family and Community Services and Housing, because there was a
tradition in these departments of employment of women in senior
grades. Therefore the comparison of departmental cultures is one way
of exploring gender inequalities in work organizations.

Chapters 5 and 6 focus directly on gender, addressing in Chapter
5 issues of women's and men's representation in union office-holding,
and in Chapter 6 the way union policy issues concerning gender were
addressed by the branch and by male and female shop stewards and
union officers. Chapter 5 charts gender variations in union office-
holding and performance of the shop steward role. The discussion is

organized in a similar way to the discussion of occupational variations in Chapter 4, so that the themes of occupational and gender variation can be compared more easily by the reader. It explores the sources of continued union activism and the relation between union activism and personal life. It is thus of particular interest to readers concerned with ways of increasing women's representation in trade unions. The influence of occupational inequalities on women's union participation is explored particularly in terms of the operation of the union facility agreement concerning time off for trade union work.

Chapter 6 looks at the policy-making and collective bargaining side of the union's work. It reports considerable support among shop stewards and union officers of both sexes for equality issues on the union's bargaining agenda. There was a strong correspondence between the national policies of the union on women's rights and the views of its activist members. The research did not identify any major gender differences among shop stewards in priorities for collective bargaining, but it did find some interesting evidence of gender differences in styles of bargaining. There was also a problem identified by senior female branch officers and stewards of managerial hostility to women union representatives, especially when they took on a negotiating role. This constitutes a problem for unions in encouraging women members to take on negotiating work.

The conclusion sums up the research findings and discusses their policy implications and directions for future research. It suggests that in order to increase women's representation within trade unions, unions should pay more attention to the operation of union facility agreements and to positive action in employment. Improving women's position with the workplace and within trade unions are part of the same process.

Chapter 2

Gender, Work and Union Activism

This chapter contains a literature review and a discussion of changes in women's position in the trade union movement. The literature review starts with a look at literature on union participation and office-holding, including the extent to which it has taken account of or ignored the influence of gender. The existing literature on gender and trade unions will then be reviewed. Finally there is an evaluation of changes in women's position in the unions in the 1970s and 1980s.

Union Participation and Office-Holding

This section will first examine some of the more common explanations of union participation and office-holding, particularly those related to work involvement, and indicate how they relate to women's union participation.

Studies of union participation often tend to focus on a number of quantifiable indices of participation, such as attending meetings, voting in union elections, filing grievances, reading union literature and holding union office (Fonow, 1977; Anderson, 1979; Fosh, 1981). There is no common definition of what is meant by union participation, which creates difficulties in studying it. Moreover, the opportunities for participation available to members vary with the structure and degree of democracy of the particular union.

Much literature on union participation (Dean, 1954; Form and Danserau, 1957; Tannenbaum and Kahn, 1958; Spinrad, 1960) emphasizes the importance of work involvement as a factor motivating union participation. Commitment to work and the recognition of work as a central life interest is seen as encouraging union activism. For women workers this approach to union participation raises the issue of how central paid work is in women's lives. It is more likely to be relevant to women workers in full-time and permanent jobs.

The commitment to work approach appeared especially relevant in the case of NALGO members. The history of NALGO shows the role of the union in creating the profession of local government officer (Spoor, 1967). NALGO campaigns in the 1980s and early 1990s focused on the theme of defending services and opposing cuts in public expenditure. The commitment to work factor may fit particularly well too in the case of a trade union like NALGO which was originally set up as a professional body for whose early national officers trade unionism was, in the words of a frequently cited quotation, 'nausea' (Spoor, 1967). Thus the concept of commitment to work and indeed of a professional orientation to work is important in explaining the history of NALGO.

The commitment to work factor may operate differently for workers at different levels of the occupational hierarchy. Obviously some workers have greater reasons than others for being committed to work, in terms of the rewards their jobs offer. Also, at some more senior levels commitment to work and advancement in the job may mean an end to union activism, given the conflicting demands on individuals' time from their job and their union work. There is also the complex relationship between union activism and promotion prospects. For some union office-holders union activism is felt to be a threat to career prospects, while for others the increased visibility to management, which occurs as a result of union involvement, can improve chances of promotion. Indeed in the study of Sheffield NALGO it appeared that more men than women were promoted out of union activism. It cannot therefore be assumed unproblematically that commitment to work is necessarily reflected in increased union activism.

There is also the question of how well this theory applies in the case of white-collar workers. Some of the literature which explains union participation in terms of work involvement (Lipset, Trow and Coleman, 1956) is clearly theorizing based on the experience of an aristocracy of labour, composed of highly skilled manual workers. Several studies of union participation do explore variations according to skill/job status, gender and white-collar/blue-collar status (Dubin, 1973; Anderson, 1979; Blyton, Nicholson and Ursell, 1981; Davis, 1981; Griffin, 1981; Nicholson, Ursell and Blyton, 1981). Variations in job status are generally found to be more significant than the blue-collar/white-collar split or gender differences (Dean, 1954), lending support to the view that commitment to work is a major factor motivating individuals towards union activism.

One of the difficulties with the commitment to work theories as an explanation of union participation is that different writers may be discussing different forms or dimensions of work commitment. These can cover areas such as job satisfaction, solidaristic or bureaucratic orientations to work, adherence to the protestant work ethic or even a negative or dissatisfied response to work. In the case of many public sector workers and other workers in service industries there is often a conflict between professional standards and bureaucratic authority and limits in public expenditure. Rose (1985), in his discussion of the work ethic, suggests that adherence to it may be a form of occupational self-interest among white-collar public sector trade unionists. He also identifies it with a strand of feminism, which emphasizes the importance of work and economic independence for women. Such a conflict between commitment to the job and the limitations of the organizational structure can produce either psychological withdrawal from work or a radical and critical form of participation in both the work organization and the trade union. This latter type of response is perhaps best seen in occupational groups such as social workers (Joyce, Corrigan and Hayes, 1988).

In developing a theory of union participation it is necessary to consider both barriers to participation and reasons for participation. There is a danger of an implicit assumption that union members ought to participate which researchers may acquire either from the union activists with whom they carry out their research or from their own personal beliefs and union activism. Literature on union participation can approach the explanation of union participation either by examining factors which motivate and encourage participation or by examining barriers to participation. It is noteworthy that the most influential explanations of women's union participation (Wertheimer and Nelson, 1975) have focused on barriers to participation while theories of men's union participation or of union participation in general have focused on reasons for participation. The significance of this will be explored in the next section.

For union activism to develop there is a need for both the absence of insuperable barriers to participation, and also the presence of effective reasons for participation. As Lipset *et al.* in *Union Democracy* (1956) point out, much research on union participation contains an implicit assumption that members ought to participate. They write:

> Instead of asking why men do not attend union meetings (a question which follows on the assumption that they should) we might ask, 'Why do they go when they do, and what kind of rewards are there for attendance?' (p. 262)

The particular relevance of this point in the case of women workers will be discussed in the next section.

Gender and Trade Unions

Studies of gender and unions, especially of women and unions, for many years consisted of far more historical studies (Goldmann, 1974; Baxandall, 1976; Cantor and Laurie, 1977; Lewenhak, 1977; Soldon, 1978; Breitenbach, 1981; Soldon, 1985; Boston, 1987) than present-day studies. Present-day academic studies and policy reports have dealt with a number of themes: women's participation in unions (Beynon and Blackburn, 1972; Wertheimer and Nelson, 1975; Fonow, 1977; Harrison, 1979; Purcell, 1979; Heritage, 1983; Cook, Lorwin and Daniels, 1984; Baden, 1986; Till-Retz, 1986; Cobble, 1990); under-representation of women in union leadership (Cook, 1968; Dewey, 1971; Bergquist, 1974; Krebs, 1975; Fryer, Fairclough and Manson, 1978; Hardman, 1984; Rees, 1990); women union leaders (Abicht, 1976; Ledgerwood, 1980; Izraeli, 1984; Walton, 1985; Roby and Uttal, 1988; Heery and Kelly, 1988a, 1988b, 1989; Ledwith *et al.*, 1990); and the responsiveness of union structures and policies to women's interests (Lorwin, 1979; Coote and Kellner, 1980; Leman, 1980; Ellis, 1981; Cunnison, 1983; Milkman, 1985; Burton, 1987; Ellis, 1988; Feldberg, 1987; Cockburn, 1991; Faue, 1991).

In this section the major research literature in the field so far will be discussed under the following headings: approaches to the study of women's union participation; under-representation of women in union office-holding; women union leaders; and responsiveness of union structures and policies to women's interests.

Approaches to the Study of Women's Union Participation

Lipset, Trow and Coleman's question 'Why do they go when they do, and what kind of rewards are there for attendance?' (Lipset *et al.*, 1956) is a particularly relevant question in the case of women union members. In the past, and still to some extent in the present, trade unions have often not paid sufficient attention to the demands and needs of women members (Lewenhak, 1977; Soldon, 1978; Boston, 1987; Colling and Dickens, 1989). Moreover many women's double workload, carrying out both paid work in employment and unpaid work in the home, makes it difficult for them to take on a third set of tasks and re-sponsibilities as a union office-holder.

The 1972 study by Beynon and Blackburn on men's and women's perceptions of work indicated two major factors affecting women's union involvement. One was the significance of the split between full-time and part-time working, with part-time workers being less involved in the union. The other major factor was the prejudices of male shop stewards who considered women uninterested in unions and often only working for pin money. In terms of Wertheimer and Nelson's (1975) study these women experienced both work-related and union-related barriers to participation.

Wertheimer and Nelson's 1975 study of women's participation in New York City locals is still the classic study of women trade unionists, referred to by most subsequent researchers. At the time, its identification of three groups of barriers to participation, work-related, union-related and cultural-societal-personal, provided a useful framework for the study of the position of women in trade unions. Much subsequent research has confirmed the importance of the various barriers to participation they identify. For instance studies concerning the under-representation of women in unions often show that it is particularly women in low-status, low-paid jobs who are under-represented in union office-holding, reinforcing the significance of the work-related group of barriers to participation. Research on women union office-holders has indicated that a large number of them are single and do not have young children, and in this respect has confirmed the significance of the cultural-societal-personal category. Discussion of how unions can become more responsive to women's concerns and interests shows that the union-related category is still relevant.

Following the influential work of Wertheimer and Nelson (1975), other studies of women's union participation have started with the examination of barriers to participation. The theoretical problem with this approach is that the removal of obstacles or barriers to participation does not of itself provide any positive reasons for participation. For instance the creation of extra leisure time through the provision of more social facilities for childcare would not necessarily mean that more parents of young children would become union activists or indeed engage in any other voluntary activity. This is a point that some of Wertheimer and Nelson's informants recognize when they note disapprovingly that non-activists find time to go to the hairdresser but not the union meeting (Wertheimer and Nelson, 1975). There can be work-related, union-related and societal-cultural-personal reasons for union participation and office-holding. Given the progress women have made in trade unions since Wertheimer and Nelson wrote in 1975 it is now appropriate for the study of women's union involvement to place more emphasis on reasons for participation, while not discounting the significance of barriers to participation for many women workers.

One study of a group of women workers who were highly committed to work is Fonow's study of women steel-workers in the USA (Fonow, 1977). These were women who had entered non-traditional jobs under affirmative action programmes. She found that women who were active in the union tended to compare their job status with that of men in the steel industry, whereas non-active women tended to compare their present jobs with their previous work. One factor Fonow identifies as a motivator for union activism was economic independence, a factor which tends to span the work-related and personal-societal-cultural dimensions of union participation. She found that the most active women tended either to be single or divorced or to be married to men with low incomes.

Harrison's 1979 study of ASTMS (Association of Scientific, Technical and Managerial Staffs) members is, despite the title, 'Participation of Women in Trade Union Activities: Some Research Findings and Comments', a comparative study of women's and men's union participation. Her research is based on a questionnaire study of ninety-six women and ninety-two men. She found that 75 per cent of the women and 63 per cent of the men never attended branch meetings. Differences in job grades were significant for both sexes, with workers on higher grades more likely to participate. The timing of union meetings affected the attendance of both men and women. The venue of the union meeting was a factor which affected women's but not men's attendance. What Harrison's study indicates is both similarities and differences in men's and women's union participation.

Purcell (1979) notes that there is a widespread assumption among writers on industrial relations and male trade unionists that women workers are less militant than men. She refers to this as the 'passive woman worker thesis'. She argues that there is a need to distinguish betwen militancy and activism, that militancy is an undefined concept and that militancy is dependent on the situation. The reason many women workers may appear less militant is that they work in industries where workers are in a weaker bargaining position and so have less opportunity for the exercise of industrial militancy. In this respect Purcell's argument focuses on work-related factors. She notes also that most active female stewards were single or did not have children and that many women workers may be put off by the homosocial, male club aspect of trade unionism.

The study of the unionization of the London clearing banks by Heritage (1977, 1983) shows the significance of occupational segregation in influencing the union participation of male and female bank workers. Banking was an industry characterized by an internal labour market in which women were brought in at lower levels, where most stayed without any career prospects or access to training, while men were brought in at a higher level and put on a career path. Thus when it came to willingness to take industrial action for union recognition, the men were more reluctant than the women, because the men, but not the women, had career prospects to lose. Heritage also notes the popularity with female bank staff of the union's demand for Saturday closing of banks, although the evidence for a major gender difference here is not convincing, since there is little evidence that the masculine gender role, apart from a few self-proclaimed workaholics, involves a strong desire to work at weekends. There is probably more gender difference in the uses to which weekend time is allocated (Green, Hebron and Woodward, 1990).

An example of the interrelationship of union-related and cultural-societal-personal barriers to participation is provided by Cook, Lorwin and Daniels (1984). They note that in some Scandanavian countries women encountered difficulties in taking on union office because of the requirement that office-holders were active both in the union and in a working-class political party, and while women could possibly have combined union or party activism with their work and domestic roles, it was impossible for many women to combine all four.

Baden (1986) argues that many past studies of union participation tended to ignore the issue of gender. This is not entirely accurate, although it is the case that many of the classic studies of the 1950s and 1960s made certain rigid assumptions about gender roles, but this was before the development of feminist writings which made a clear distinction between sex and gender (Oakley, 1972). Baden notes that an increase in female membership and leadership in public sector unions occurred at the time of the growth of the women's movement, and that many women in public sector unions were motivated to take up union office as a result of feminist politics.

Till-Retz (1986) argues that in Europe the major progress in women's involvement in unions occurred after the mid 1970s. Like Baden's, her analysis suggests that feminism has had a considerable impact on women's union participation and that unions have to some degree responded by making room for women within union structures, for example through the establishment of women's rights committees and reserved places for women on union leadership bodies. It is noticeable that the more recent studies, while acknowledging that much still has to be done for women to be equal in unions, present a rather more 'optimistic' picture of women's levels of union participation. This underlines the need for studies of women's union participation to avoid starting off from an assumption that women participate less than men, and to be careful to research reasons for participation as well as barriers to participation.

The study by Cobble (1990) of union organization among waitresses in the USA is one instance of a study which takes as its focus the explanation of high levels of union activism among women. Waitresses organized in HERE (Hotel Employees and Restaurant Employees) International Union were well organized and often took on union leadership roles. This arose partly because of work-related factors in that waitressing as a job developed skills of negotiating, controlling situations and answering back to customers, which made it easier for women to participate in debate at union meetings. Waitresses also tended to belong to an occupational community in which they socialized with other waitresses especially when working split shifts, often shared accommodation with other waitresses, and had a pride in the job. Some similarities can be seen with the printworkers studied by Lipset, Trow and Coleman (1956), who had a strong sense of occupational identity and socialized with other printworkers, especially in the early years in the trade when they worked the night shift. The personal domestic situation of many waitresses also meant they did not experience family-related barriers to union participation. Many waitresses were single, divorced, separated or widowed and so were not in traditional family situations, which made union participation easier.

Lastly the union structure encouraged, indeed forced, women's union participation. Many waitresses were organized in single-sex locals and so had no option but to take on union office-holding, if they wanted a union to represent them. The single-sex structure of the locals arose largely from occupational segregation in the industry. The majority of female leaders at the national level too tended to come from single-sex locals and the highest level of women's participation in the union occurred in the 1920s when the majority of women were in single-sex locals. The female locals declined from the 1930s, but women's committees were created in the new mixed locals to encourage women's participation, although their effectiveness was limited. Cobble notes that a combination of work-related, family-related and union-related circumstances created high and enduring patterns of union activism among waitresses in an AFL-affiliated craft union, an area not traditionally considered favourable to women's union representation.

Women's Under-Representation in Union Office-Holding

There is a substantial body of literature which documents women's under-representation in trade union leadership (Cook, 1968; Dewey, 1971; Bergquist, 1974; Krebs, 1975; Fryer, Fairclough and Manson, 1978; Hardman, 1984; Rees, 1990). It should be kept in mind that participation and representation are not the same. It is perfectly possible for women to participate, especially at the local levels, without achieving high union office. For instance Hardman notes that in her study of a GMWU (General and Municipal Workers' Union) branch women were a majority of the members and of the shop stewards, but the men held the most important union offices. Moreover the men had introduced a rule into the branch so that whenever there was a female convenor, she had to have a male deputy, and vice versa. This form of reserved places for men had been brought in to avoid a situation in which women held both the convenor and deputy convenor posts (Hardman, 1984).

The work of Fryer, Fairclough and Manson (1978) is one of the most important studies of the processes whereby women come to be under-represented in union leaderships. In their study of NUPE (National Union of Public Employees) they found that women members, particularly in Local Authority Education Departments, were disadvantaged in union office-holding by being part-time workers. Being part-time, they were not in the workplace all day and so it was harder for them to represent members. Moreover, full-time jobs, such as school caretaker, which were more likely to be be performed by men, pro-vided access to an office, telephone and photocopier, thus supplying resources which made it easier to be a union representative. This study showed the need for unions to negotiate facilities agreements, which provide both part-time and full-time workers with access to office space and equipment and paid time off for union work. Fryer *et al.* recommend that unions seeking to improve women's levels of office-holding need to pay more attention to the operation of facility agree-ments. Their work is significant in terms of highlighting the influence of occupational factors on women's union participation.

Rees (1990) examines women's union participation and represen-tation in NALGO and USDAW (Union of Shop, Distributive and Allied Workers). She links these issues with the issue of union demo-cracy. Her explanation for women's under-representation in union office-holding in both unions involves factors arising from women's work and family situation. In terms of work-related factors, women worked in lower-status occupations, had interrupted working lives and were more likely to work part-time. This led to shorter periods of continuous union membership, which made women less likely to take on union office. Also she found that while the typical male NALGO activist was married with young children, the typical female activist was more likely to be single and childfree than NALGO women members in general.

Handwritten margin notes: Internal? Flexible working the culprit?

Women Union Leaders

Given all the literature dealing with the obstacles to women's union participation and the under-representation of women in union leadership, what is known about women union leaders at local and national level? The study of women who do rise to union leadership is important for understanding women's union involvement in general. A small but increasing body of literature on women lay officers and full-time officials indicates two trends, namely that most are single and do not have young children, and many are to some degree influenced by feminism.

The significance of personal situation is indicated in the research of Abicht (1976), who in a comparative study of Belgium and the USA found that women union office-holders were more likely to be single, self-supporting and without children. Ledgerwood (1980) in her study of 255 CLUW (Coalition of Labor Union Women) members found that over half were single. Walton (1985) in her study of shop stewards in the Kent County branch of NALGO records that more male than female stewards had young children. She notes that her results corresponded too with the national survey of NALGO members by Rees and Reed (1981) which found that more male stewards tended to be maried and more female stewards to be single. The study of women full-time officials by Heery and Kelly (1988a, 1989) notes that 54 per cent of their informants did not have children. Ledwith *et al.* (1990) in their study of women in SOGAT (Society of Graphical and Allied Trades) present a slightly more complex view of the presence of children. They found that many women union leaders did not have children or had grown-up children, but they found a small minority who were seeking to combine working, raising small children and union office-holding. Such women were very dependent on support of partners, mothers and childminders.

Roby and Uttal (1988) provide the most detailed discussion of the relationship for male and female stewards between home life and union office-holding. They conducted 124 in-depth interviews with shop stewards, 47 per cent of whom were female. The male stewards were more likely to be married with children. Eighteen per cent of male stewards and 27 per cent of female stewards were single. They found that single female stewards were more active in the union than single male stewards, while married male stewards were more active than married female stewards. So marriage appeared to increase men's levels of union activism, but to decrease women's. They found that while both men and women experienced problems of combining family and union life, they had different problems and reached different solutions. The female stewards in their survey who were married and had children tended to reduce their union work outside work time and prioritized family commitments, such as children's birthday parties. The male stewards who were married more often allowed union work to spill over into non-work time and prioritized union commitments over family ones. Clearly they relied on the fact that their wife would be present at the children's birthday parties, although Roby and Uttal point out that many of the wives of male stewards were themselves in full-time paid employment. One male steward even chose to go picketing rather than be present at the birth of his child. For many female stewards the solution to pressures of union work was to cut back on time spent in personal relationships, to get divorced from husbands who were not prepared to accept their union involvement, and to negotiate carefully the terms of any new relationships they entered.

The impact of feminist ideas on women union office-holders is shown in Heery and Kelly (1988b). They explored the negotiating priorities of union full-time officials, and found that many women full-time officials, especially the more recently appointed ones, as well as a significant minority of male full-time officials, had been influenced by feminism and did consider equal opportunities issues as important parts of the union's bargaining agenda. They identified the promotion of women's interests as an important part of their job. It was an aspect of the work to which they felt a strong personal commitment and from which they derived considerable job satisfaction.

Other studies of women in union leadership give some indication of how women reach union office and how they participate in union committees. Cunnison (1983) and Ledwith *et al.* (1990) indicate the importance of sponsorship in the acquisition of union office. Both studies note the tendency of some existing senior office-holders, usually men, to encourage women to take on union positions, although Ledwith *et al.* note that some women manage to get elected to positions in the union without sponsorship. Izraeli's study of gender proportions on union committees in Israel looks at ways in which gender inequality persists (Izraeli, 1984). She employs Kanter's concept of tilted groups (Kanter, 1977) to examine men's and women's attitudes on union committees which varied in gender balance. Kanter's analysis of inequalities in employment focuses particularly on ratios of minority and majority categories, starting with the token situation, in which only a few women or members of ethnic minorities are hired and so experience the stresses of being on trial on behalf of their section of humanity. Then, as the proportion of the minority within the group reaches 15 per cent, Kanter defines it as a skewed group. Once the minority has reached 35 per cent she defines it as a tilted group. While similar processes of stereotyping occur within skewed and tilted groups, they are stronger in skewed groups.

Izraeli's study is concerned with tilted groups (the 35:65 per cent ratio), some tilted in favour of men and others tilted in favour of women. She finds that women felt more influential when women were in a majority on a committee, but men felt more influential when they were in a minority on a committee. She argues therefore that the election of women to union office does not necessarily guarantee that they will occupy leading positions on committees. In this respect her conclusions are similar to those of Hardman (1984). This study suggests that even women who have been elected onto union committees still encounter barriers to participation, which fall into the personal-societal-cultural category of Wertheimer and Nelson (1975).

Responsiveness of Union Structures and Policies to Women's Interests

Wertheimer and Nelson's discussion of union-related barriers to women's participation indicates the significance of the structure and culture of unions as collective organizations in terms of women's union involvement. This raises the question of how far unions have changed as the number of women members and office-holders has increased. This is partly a matter of policies and bargaining priorities, partly a matter of ways of organizing. As Lorwin (1979) notes, these developments require changes on the part of men as well as women. He quotes one of his male informants as saying: 'The only correct answer to the question, "What shall we do about women?" is "We must do something about men"'.

The 1980 report by Coote and Kellner criticized trade unions for failing to respond to the needs of women members in terms of both bargaining priorities and the operation of union structures. Their study was written at a time when the impact of feminism on the trade union movement was very uneven. The study by Leman (1980) of developments in the women's rights work of three unions — ACTT, NALGO and NATFHE shows that considerable progress was made in some unions during the 1970s. She notes that until the 1970s the trade union agenda on women's rights was largely confined to equality in terms of pay, pensions and other job-related benefits.

Leman's account shows how the range of issues unions considered as part of their women's rights policy expanded in response to the debates about abortion rights and around the Working Women's Charter, which took place in the 1970s. (These developments are discussed later in this chapter.) Ellis (1981) also indicates that several unions did make major changes in the 1970s, conducting much action research into the position of women in the union and in employment and developing new structures to address women's issues. Ellis (1981) explains women's under-representation in unions largely in terms of the same factors which make for women's under-achievement in employment, i.e. occupational segregation and domestic responsibilities. Consequently her later work (1988) addresses the limited success trade unions have had in tackling occupational segregation, while recognizing the extent of change within the trade union movement.

Gender differences may exist not only in bargaining priorities, but also in styles of collective bargaining and union organizing. Cunnison (1983) discusses the failure of union branch structures to address the problems faced by female school meals staff, when the women went to the meeting and tried to raise matters of concern to them. Because the women did not know how to operate union procedures they were unable to get their issues onto the agenda and left the meeting feeling frustrated and angry. This example raises the question of the balance between on the one hand educating women to participate more effectively in unions as they are presently structured and on the other changing the structures of unions to make them more accessible to women members. Milkman (1985) compares the examples of CLUW (Coalition of Labor Union Women) and the National Organization of Working Women: 9 to 5 as alternative ways of organizing women workers.

CLUW was established in 1974 at a founding convention in Chicago attended by 3,000 women from fifty-eight different labour unions. Its membership is restricted to existing union members. The first convention adopted four goals: organizing unorganized women;

working in unions to win support for affirmative action; involving more union women in political campaigns such as support for the Equal Rights Amendment; encouraging women's participation within unions. Milkman argues that despite these goals CLUW has increasingly come to focus on helping women who are already in the unions to move upwards in the union structures. CLUW in 1985 had 15,000 members with sixty local chapters. It provided training and empowerment to help women get on in the existing union structures. Its keenest members were full-time union employees, who found that it provided a valuable network. Milkman suggests that CLUW's practice is quite individualistic and so the organization may be difficult for rank-and-file women members and unorganized women to identify with.

Milkman argues that a very different form of women's union organizing is represented by the National Organization of Working Women: 9 to 5, which draws far more from feminist than from traditional trade union ways of organizing. It was originally established in Boston in 1973 as an organization for women office workers outside labour unions. It started with consciousness-raising and organizing around specific issues affecting office workers such as sexual harassment at work and unsafe office technology. Effectively it became a pre-union organization, which brought into collective action groups of office workers who did not see unions as relevant to them and were not necessarily prepared to join a union immediately.

Another similar organization to 9 to 5 was Union WAGE (Union Women's Alliance to Gain Equality). This was a newspaper for working women established in 1971 in San Francisco. It existed until 1982 and provided an organizing focus for rank-and-file women unionists. It viewed CLUW as too closely tied to the official labour movement and believed that CLUW's practice of only recruiting women who were already union members excluded the 90 per cent of US women wage-earners who were not unionized, including many third world women who worked in low-paid and non-unionized jobs (Downing, 1984).

Burton (1987) gives a similar account to Milkman of the Baltimore Working Women Group which later affiliated to 9 to 5. In 1975, 9 to 5 received a charter from the Service Employees' International Union and began organizing SEIU Local 925. Thus there developed two organizations, one an independent campaigning organization of women office workers, the National Organization of Working Women: 9 to 5, and one which is within the organized labour movement, SEIU District 925. SEIU District 925 places much of its focus on organizing all unorganized women clerical workers in the USA. It enjoys a considerable degree of autonomy within SEIU. Milkman (1985) quotes the

SEIU President as saying that District 925 was to be run 'for women and by women who understand their problems'.

Thus SEIU District 925 is starting its union organizing from one feminist perspective that women are different from men, have different priorities and needs in labour organizations and different ways of organizing, whereas CLUW is working from another feminist perspective that men and women essentially have common interests as workers and that, in the words of the CLUW slogan, 'a woman's place is in her union'. Milkman (1985) argues that both CLUW and 9 to 5 are examples of the impact of feminism on the union movement. She writes:

> In contrast to CLUW's focus on 'empowerment', 9 to 5 rejects the traditional 'macho' image of unionism, insisting that women workers, unaccustomed to viewing themselves as powerful, will be successfully unionised only if a different, more woman-oriented culture of unionism is developed. (p. 316)

The question of union culture comes up in a number of studies. Heery and Kelly (1989) found that three-quarters of their sample of women full-time union officers agreed that 'a woman union officer has to be tough to be successful at her job'. Some equated toughness with dedication and never going off sick unless very ill. For others toughness meant the development of a hard macho style, especially in negotiations. The fact that women full-time officers found it necessary to adopt these 'masculine' standards of behaviour did not mean they approved of them, wished to conform to them or considered them appropriate when working with women members. They were simply viewed as necessary survival mechanisms.

Feldberg (1987), Cockburn (1991) and Faue (1991) argue that the failure of unions to incorporate 'women's culture' has been a major factor in the labour movement's lack of success in organizing women workers. The argument that unions need to focus more on women's workplace culture is an argument that unions need to pay more attention to gender differences when organizing women workers.

Much of the discussion of how far unions have adapted to become more relevant and more welcoming to women members in the 1970s rests upon some rather tenuous assumptions about what women members want from unions and how women view their work and their union situation. This involves several issues: how far women and men are similar or different in their priorities for collective bargaining and their preferred styles of union organizing; how far women have common interests and to what degree women have different interests according to job status, class, race, ethnicity and similar divisions; how trade unions as organizations both recognize and respond to membership heterogeneity and maintain a basis of united action. The relationship between diversity and unity is a political problem which has also been addressed in the women's movement (Hamilton and Barrett, 1987; Ramazanoglu, 1989).

Within trade unions it has to be recognized that all women will not have the same bargaining agenda or preferred styles of union organizing. Milkman's comparative analysis of CLUW and 9 to 5 is an example of this (Milkman, 1985). Among women workers it is possible that full-time and part-time, permanent and temporary workers may have different policy priorities. Some women workers may be comfortable with traditional, formal union styles of organizing, while some may prefer more informal women's movement ways of running meetings. Some women workers may wish to see unions become more feminist in policies and ways of working, while others may reject anything that is overtly feminist. It is also important to recognize that women workers often share many bargaining priorities with their male colleagues, particularly those relating to conditions of service and the problem of low pay.

Trade Union Policies on Women's Rights

During the 1970s and early 1980s many trade unions developed policies and issued pamphlets on equal rights for women (General and Municipal Workers Union, 1976; Society of Civil and Public Servants, 1982). Many unions too have supported working parties and research into the position of women in the industry and the union (Fryer, Fairclough and Manson, 1978; NALGO, 1975, 1980; Rees and Reed, 1981; Ledwith *et al.*, 1990). In this section the development of trade union policies on women's rights is explored under four subheadings: equal pay, the Working Women's Charter Campaign, abortion rights and positive action. These changes arose in part from the increasing number of women in trade unions, from feminist campaigning within the unions, increases in the number of women holding union office and the impact of European Community laws and the discussion around the proposed Social Charter (NALGO and the European Network of Women, n.d.).

Equal Pay

It is widely accepted in the trade union movement that its record in fighting for equal pay for women has not been commendable, with little action following the adoption of a resolution in 1888 at the TUC calling for equal pay. The attachment of many trade unions to the concept of the family wage (Barrett and McIntosh, 1980) undermined their ability to fight effectively for equal pay, and it is noteworthy that the unions which achieved equal pay earliest for their members (unions representing teachers and civil servants) were ones which had traditionally organized single women workers, because of the existence of a marriage bar in teaching and the civil service between the two world wars (Lewenhak, 1977; Beale, 1982; Boston, 1987).

The 1968 strike of Ford's machinists at Dagenham was a dispute over pay grading, which became an equal pay dispute and led to the passing of the 1970 Equal Pay Act (Friedman and Meredeen, 1980). When the Equal Pay Act came into force at the end of 1975 many tribunal cases were taken on equal pay and a few significant strikes occurred.

The actions by many trade unions in supporting members taking equal value cases (e.g. GMB and Julie Hayward *v.* Cammell Laird) showed the continuing significance of the equal pay issue for women workers. Similarly in the USA the issue of pay equity has been the most important women's issue in the public sector unions (Bell, 1985; Baden, 1986). Pay equity is a concept which is similar to the demand for equal pay for work of equal value. Thus unlike affirmative action strategies which seek to obtain entry for women into non-traditional, better-paid jobs, pay equity campaigns seek to improve women's position in employment by revaluing and upgrading the jobs women currently perform.

In Britain the complexity of the equal value regulations means that an equal value case can take several years to resolve, and so taking up equal pay via collective bargaining can still be a more effective and attractive option for women workers (Labour Research Department, 1989; NUPE, n.d.).

What is significant in trade unions' record over the issues of equal pay and low pay has been their willingness to rely on the law and to permit legal intervention in women's wages (trade boards and wages councils) and hours of work. As Boston (1987) notes, the tradition of voluntarism and the belief of unions in free collective bargaining has never applied to women workers. Nonetheless the equal pay victories at Ford's and at Trico-Folberth were achieved by women workers through taking industrial action.

The Working Women's Charter Campaign

Leman (1980) notes in her study of the development of the women's rights work of ACTT, NALGO and NATFHE that unions tended to be concerned with equal pay for a very long period before they developed a wider agenda on women's rights. One development in the 1970s which contributed to a qualitative widening of trade unions' agenda on women's rights was the Working Women's Charter Campaign. The Working Women's Charter was a ten-point programme on women's rights at work and in society, which was adopted by a sub-committee of the London Trades Council in 1974. It was never formally adopted by the whole Trades Council because it was reorganized before it took a position on the Charter. What was innovatory about the Working Women's Charter was the linking of demands relating to the workplace and to women's position in society generally, thus widening the traditional trade union agenda on women's rights and to some degree incorporating a feminist analysis of women's inequality at work.

The Working Women's Charter was adopted as policy by many trades councils and trade unions, often following conferences discussing its demands (Lawrence, 1977; Boston, 1987). NALGO adopted it as policy at its 1975 Conference (Leman, 1980). The 1975 TUC Conference did not adopt the Charter, because of objections at that time to the principle of a national minimum wage, although a later version of the Charter was issued by the TUC. There was also some objection to the Charter because it referred to abortion rights, although the same TUC Conference had also adopted policy opposing the James White Anti-Abortion Bill (Hunt and Adams, 1980; Cockburn, 1984). The principle of a national minimum wage was supported by TUC conferences in the late 1980s, being particularly advocated by unions such as NUPE which represented many low-paid women workers. The change in policy on the national minimum wage question arose not simply as a result of greater trade union sensitivity to women's demands, however, but also as a result of the weakened bargaining position of many unions.

Abortion Rights

The debates over abortion rights in the unions in the late 1970s established the principle that abortion was a trade union issue. Many unions at branch, regional and national level adopted policies opposing anti-abortion legislation and supporting the defence of the 1967 Abortion Act and the principle of women's right to choose. NALGO passed a resolution to this effect at its 1978 Annual Conference (NALGO, n.d. (a)). In 1979 the TUC called a demonstration against the Corrie Anti-Abortion Bill. This was the first time in the world that a major trade union federation had called a demonstration on abortion rights (Beale, 1982). More recently in 1989 in the USA there were demonstrations against any moves in the Supreme Court to reverse Roe *v.* Wade, the legal case which in practice allowed abortion on request in the first trimester, with labour unionists participating in the demonstrations carrying placards saying 'pro-union, pro-choice'.

Seven trade unions in Britain, including NALGO, affiliated to the National Abortion Campaign, a pro-choice organization set up in 1975 to oppose the James White Abortion (Amendment) Bill, which aimed to restrict the operation of the 1967 Abortion Act. Trade union support was also strong in the 1987/88 campaign against the Alton Bill, with many unions issuing leaflets and posters for lobbies and demonstrations and financing coaches, enabling members to attend demonstrations.

Support for women's abortion rights was an important development in union policies on women's rights, since it involved explicit recognition that women could not be equal in the workplace without fertility control. It was a culmination of the development of an understanding that the trade union agenda had to incorporate demands relating to women's position in society as well as in the workplace, for real equality for women to be achieved. This was to some degree the result of the debates which had taken place in the unions around the Working Women's Charter and feminist ideas generally.

Positive Action

Increasing union interest in the concept of positive action arose both from an appreciation that legislation (the 1970 Equal Pay Act, the 1975 Sex Discrimination Act, the 1984 Equal Pay Amendment Act and the 1986 Sex Discrimination Amendment Act) had done little to raise the level of women's pay or to gain entry for women into better-paid and better-quality jobs, and from studying the US experience of affirmative action (Labour Research Department, 1988b). Affirmative action in the USA permits preferential hiring of women and ethnic minorities and the use of quotas in employment. The TUC in 1980 held a conference on positive action and adopted policy positions in support of it (TUC, 1986). Many individual unions, too, adopted policies in support of positive action (Banking, Insurance and Finance Union, n.d.; NALGO, n.d. (b)).

At the end of the 1970s and in the 1980s there was an increasing focus on equal opportunities as a negotiating issue. After a decade of feminist campaigning within the unions to persuade fellow union members of the justice and importance of various policies on women's rights, there developed an increasing recognition that progressive policies on equal rights needed to be turned into collective agreements. This in turn led to the understanding of the need for more women lay officers and full-time officials and for a higher level of involvement of female members in the negotiating work of the union. Beale (1982) notes the virtual absence of women from national negotiations. Women's proportionate representation in the union movement came to be seen not simply as an issue of fairness and representativeness, but also as important in terms of bargaining effectiveness. This meant too that women need to be in union posts concerned with collective bargaining as well as policy-making, educational and welfare work, where women had tended to be concentrated. The significance of an increasing number of women full-time officials being employed by trade unions has been explored by Heery and Kelly (1988b) who conclude that many women full-time officials, as well as a significant minority of male full-time officials, do attach a higher level of priority to women's issues in collective bargaining.

Women's Representation in the Trade Union Movement

Increase in Numbers of Women Trade Unionists

Women in 1990 were 34 per cent of the membership of TUC-affiliated unions and 48 per cent of the employed workforce (Labour Research Department, 1991). Underlying the changes in policies on women's rights has been the growth in female membership of trade unions. Cockburn (1987) states that the number of women trade union members grew from 1.7 million in 1968 to 3.5 million in 1978. This development affected some unions dramatically. Hunt and Adams (1980) indicate that between 1968 and 1978 there was a rapid growth in female membership of a number of unions, most noticeably ASTMS, where female membership increased by 721 per cent. For NALGO during this period female membership increased by 141 per cent.

At the level of trades union federations these changes were noticed and the need to develop policies appreciated. For instance in 1978 the Executive Board of the ICFTU (International Confederation of Free Trade Unions) adopted a programme 'Equality for Women in Trade Unions: A Programme of Action for the Integration of Women into Trade Union Organizations'. In 1985 this programme was updated by the ICFTU's Women's Committee. It emphasizes the responsibilities of unions to encourage women's participation, for example by convenient timing of union meetings, and to take steps to ensure that women are given adequate access to union training and are properly represented on union executives. Trebilcock (1991) notes that over one-third of national affiliates of the ICFTU now have reserved seats for women on their executive bodies.

In 1979 the British TUC adopted a 'Charter for Equality for Women within Trade Unions'. A 1984 TUC pamphlet incorporating this charter addressed the same issues in some detail. It included guidelines on seeing that women are adequately represented on union executives, that advisory committees on women's issues are established, that meetings are held at times convenient for parents or that childcare is provided at meetings, and that the content of union journals and publications must be presented in a non-sexist way. The TUC Charter was updated in 1990 to include targets and if necessary quotas for proportionate representation of women on union decision-making bodies (Labour Research Department, 1991). Within the European Community there has been increased interest on the part of the European TUC and various trade union federations to increase women's representation, but there has also been some opposition to special measures such as reserved places and women are still under-represented (Labour Research Department, 1990b).

Actions to Overcome Barriers to Participation

For many unions overcoming barriers to participation constituted one of the main starting points for improving women's participation in the union. The barriers identified were often childcare/domestic responsibilities and sexism within the unions. In many unions the case was won for the provision of creches at union meetings or the payment of babysitting expenses where more appropriate. Where possible unions attempted to hold meetings in working hours, but a union generally has to be in a strong bargaining position to persuade an employer to allow paid time off work for union meetings. Moreover, as Beale (1982) notes, holding the union meeting in the lunch hour does not necessarily assist women's participation, if they usually use the lunch hour to do shopping.

Sometimes, too, the venue of a union meeting has been identified as a barrier to women's participation (Harrison, 1979). Many women do not feel comfortable attending meetings in public houses or in certain parts of town which are unsafe to walk in or travel to by public transport, especially after dark. This may be especially the case for black women, who also face the danger of racial harassment. There has been some growing awareness on the part of unions that such practices need changing, but they still occur. The type of venue adjourned to after the meeting may also be significant. In 1974 (before the passing of the Sex Discrimination Act in 1975) as a representative from Newcastle Working Women's Charter Group I went to speak to a meeting of the Newcastle Branch of the Inland Revenue Staff Federation. It was an evening meeting held in union offices in the centre of Newcastle. Two women members were present at an overwhelmingly male meeting. The male members of the branch were genuinely keen to encourage more women to be active in the union. Unfortunately, however, it was the practice of the male members of that branch after the meeting to adjourn to a men-only public house. What was interesting was that they made no connection between this practice and the lack of women at the branch meetings.

Various measures were taken to overcome overt sexism in the conduct of union business, for instance many unions rewrote their rule books, deleting references to the member as 'he' and instead using non-sexist and inclusive language. NALGO did this in 1982. NALGO also issued a leaflet 'Watch Your Language', giving practical guidance on how to avoid sexist language at work and in the conduct of union meetings. This leaflet acknowledges that in the past NALGO publications were guilty of various sexist practices. For instance the NALGO magazine *Public Service* used to have a 'prettiest new recruit' competition, a practice which was discontinued in 1975 (NALGO, n.d. (h)).

Developing Women's Rights Structures Within the Unions

During the 1970s and 1980s in many unions women's rights committees at national, regional and local levels were established or reactivated. This arose partly as a result of feminist pressures within the unions, partly as a result of the increasing female membership of unions and partly perhaps from some unions' desire to recruit more women members. Within NALGO in March 1977 the NEC (National Executive Committee) set up a National Discrimination Committee, which later became renamed the National Equal Opportunities Committee. It had fifteen members, three from the NEC and one from each of the twelve districts. By 1979 district equal opportunities committees had been set up in twelve districts. The National Equal Opportunities Committee met four times a year and campaigned on childcare, equality of opportunity and monitoring progress on the implementation of the 1975 Equal Rights Working Party Report (Leman, 1980). In 1988 NALGO reorganized its equal opportunities work to establish four national committees, one for women members, one for members with disabilities, one for lesbian and gay members, and one for black and ethnic minority members (*NALGO News*, 25 November 1988).

In Britain space was made for women within the official structures, with many unions creating new advisory structures to consider policy issues of specific interest to women members (Hunt and Adams, 1980). In the USA the absence of such provision led to the formation of CLUW (Coalition of Labor Union Women) outside the official union structure. There was also the development of pre-union organizations, such as the National Organization of Working Women: 9 to 5, as mentioned earlier, one of whose groups later became District 925 affiliated to Service Employees' International Union (Burton, 1987).

Encouraging Women's Participation and Representation

Along with the establishment of policy structures to deal with women's rights issues went an increased concern to promote union office-holding by women. Unions recognized that their arguments to employers for equal opportunities were not very credible if the unions were as male-dominated as the employment structures they were criticizing. Some unions also undertook equal opportunities monitoring of women's levels of office-holding within the union.

Trebilcock (1991) reviews a variety of strategies adopted for strengthening women's participation in trade union leadership. These include developments in union policies, changing the union culture and adopting a number of structural changes. Among these structural changes has been the growing use of reserved places on union leadership bodies. Trebilcock notes that the experience of a quota system in some countries has also led to increased representation of women on bodies for which there are no quotas.

There are arguments for and against reserved places, as there are

33

for quotas in employment. Some trade unionists, both male and female, argue that reserved places are undemocratic, in that all members
should have an equal chance of election and voters should not be
required to vote for a minimum number of women candidates; they
can also be seen as patronizing because women can and ought to get
elected on their own merits. Other trade unionists, male and female,
argue that reserved places should be supported, at least on a temporary
basis, as a necessary measure to overcome prejudice and to ensure
adequate representation of women within unions.

Besides the use of reserved places, unions have employed a number
of strategies to increase women's participation, such as women-only
training courses, publicity, and prioritization of bargaining issues of
particular interest to women. While women are still under-represented
as union office-holders, especially at the more senior levels, in many
unions enough women are in a position of influence to make sure that
women's demands are less neglected than they have been in the past.

NALGO was one of the unions most affected by these changes in
the position of women in the union movement in the 1970s and 1980s.
The increase in women members' involvement in the union meant
that women played a prominent part in the 1989 NALGO national
strike and appreciated the significance of defending national pay
bargaining and conditions of service.

Conclusion

During the 1970s and 1980s there was a qualitative change in the
position of women in trade unions. There was an increase in female
membership of trade unions, a growth in women's representation in
positions of trade union leadership, and a widening of the trade union
agenda on women's rights. These changes were largely a product of
the women's liberation movement and the popular struggles of the
period. There was also a modest growth in academic literature concerning trade union women, which dealt with issues of policy and
representation. This chapter has addressed the context of the study of
Sheffield NALGO members in terms of the issues of gender and trade
unions. Chapter 3 will map out the national and local industrial relations context.

Chapter 3

Background to the Study

A Short History of NALGO

NALGO was established in 1905 with 5,000 members, from a merger of the Liverpool Municipal Officers' Guild, the London Municipal Officers' Association and other municipal officers' associations. One of its early leaders was Herbert Blain, who had established the Liverpool Municipal Officers' Guild in 1896. Blain was the first Chairman of NALGO and later became Principal Agent of the Conservative Party between 1924 and 1927 (Maybin, 1980). According to Spoor (1967), in the early years much of NALGO's work was concerned with organizing social activities for the members, such as rifle clubs, sports clubs, and holiday and motoring clubs, as well as establishing a building society and a savings and insurance society. He notes that the Sheffield Guild originally developed from a rifle club. NALGO's later radicalism and progressive stance on a whole range of questions thus developed from its beginnings as a fairly conservative occupational association.

Early leaders of NALGO tended to be conservative professionals who insisted that NALGO was not a trade union. Levi Hill, NALGO's first full-time General Secretary, stated in 1911 that 'anything savouring of trade unionism is nausea to the local government officer and his Association' (Maybin, 1980).

According to Spoor, NALGO started to become a trade union at the 1918 conference when a motion was carried calling for the establishment of a national salary scale. This conference also carried a motion calling on officers not to apply for posts in local authorities which treated their employees badly. The boycott of posts was a long-lasting NALGO tactic, with details of posts to be boycotted regularly listed in NALGO publications. In 1920 the NALGO conference voted in favour of becoming a union. Spoor suggests this was partly because NALGO was losing members among radicalized ex-soldiers who were joining rival organizations and partly because many Labour-controlled local councils were prepared to employ only trade unionists. The establishment of the Whitley Council system in 1920 did not, as NALGO had hoped, lead to the creation of national salary scales for local government. It was not until 1944 that NALGO achieved national salary scales. Meanwhile NALGO had done much to create the profession of local government officer.

Several studies of the growth of white-collar unionism note the links between unionization and bureaucratization. On the one hand growing bureaucracy and rationalization can be a factor motivating white-collar workers to join unions (Lumley, 1973), but equally on the other hand the union can be a promoter of rationalization and bureaucratization, by pushing for standardized entry criteria, grading structures and national salary scales. Lockwood (1958) and Spoor (1967) argue that NALGO played a major role in the bureaucratization of local government. The establishment of a bureaucratic structure then favours the further development of union organization, including national structures for collective bargaining. NALGO thus provides a clear illustration of some of the major theories concerning the growth of white-collar unionism.

The subsequent evolution of NALGO can also be studied as an example of the increasing radicalization of white-collar unions. In 1964 NALGO affiliated to the TUC. While the affiliation was supported by the union's leadership for largely instrumental reasons, it is reasonable to suppose that a proportion of the activists who lobbied for affiliation did so because they wanted to identify with the wider labour movement.

During the 1960s and 1970s sections of NALGO's membership experienced a degree of radicalization in relation to the content of their work. The formation of Case Con, an organization of radical social workers critical of existing social work practice, is one example of this process (Maybin, 1980; Joyce, Corrigan and Hayes, 1988). The first actual strikes of NALGO members also took place among social workers in 1978, although NALGO members in the electricity industry had voted for strike action as early as 1965 (Spoor, 1967). In 1978–79 there was a forty-two-week-long strike of social workers. The dispute was over the right of NALGO to negotiate social work grades locally. This strike paved the way for the development of far more workplace union organization and the growth of the shop steward system in NALGO. NALGO conference in 1976 supported the development of a shop steward system, a move which had been campaigned for by the Nalgo Action Group, a left-wing caucus within the union. The 1978–79 strike was followed in 1983 by a major dispute involving residential social workers (Joyce, Corrigan and Hayes, 1988). Since then NALGO branches have been involved in a number of local strikes (Weinstein, 1986).

One of the noteworthy features of this radicalization process is the imitation of blue-collar industrial forms of union organization and the link between the growth of the shop steward system and the demand for more local bargaining. In the late 1980s and early 1990s the push for plant bargaining has come more frequently from the employers' side, with national bargaining being criticized for inflexibility and lack of sensitivity to local labour market conditions. In other periods, however, it has been the trade union side which has supported workplace bargaining, as in the case of shop stewards at British Leyland in the 1970s or social workers in local government in the 1978/79 strike. Neither position, support for national or for local bargaining, is necessarily in itself more radical. For the union side the advantages of national bargaining lie in the unifying character of national salary rates and national agreements on conditions of service and the protection afforded thereby to the least well organized members, while the advantages of local bargaining are a higher level of involvement of members in workplace trade union activity, greater union democracy and the possibility of obtaining more favourable settlements for well organized groups of workers. In 1989 NALGO took national strike action for the first time in opposition to proposals from the employer to move away from national bargaining, because national rates of pay and conditions of service were seen by many trade unionists in the context of the late 1980s as gains of the labour movement which should be defended.

Another aspect of radicalization which affected NALGO, along with many other unions, in the 1970s was the growth in official union support for a number of left-wing causes, including affiliation to the Chile Solidarity Campaign, the Anti-Apartheid Movement, the Anti-Nazi League and the National Abortion Campaign (Maybin, 1980). The growing female membership of NALGO was reflected in the report in 1975 of an equal rights working party and the adoption of a range of policies on women's rights.

The issue of campaigning against cutbacks in public expenditure was also a major focus of public sector union activity over this period. Weinstein (1986) discusses the later conflicts that arose between NALGO and Labour councils over the issues of public expenditure cuts. In the 1970s and early 1980s NALGO members and Labour councils could often act jointly in campaigns against government cuts in public expenditure, even to the point of local government workers taking symbolic one-day strike actions in support of their employers against central government policies. Many NALGO members strongly identified with the cause of local government, since NALGO had done much historically to create the profession of local government officer. Many NALGO activists had a political preference for working in the public sector rather than for a private employer and to some degree believed in the practice of municipal socialism and the theory that the local state could have a degree of independence from the central state machinery to pursue socialist policies in opposition to those of a Conservative government.

The collapse of the campaign against rate-capping in the mid 1980s and the increasing recognition by Labour councils that they could not maintain all services and 'no-redundancy' policies meant the end of the road for illusions in municipal socialism. Increasingly groups of local authority trade unionists, including NALGO members, found themselves taking industrial action against Labour local authorities, and as Weinstein (1986) notes they then found themselves being accused of being variously anti-socialist, anti-working-class, racist and led by the Socialist Workers' Party. Left Labour councillors did not see industrial action by their employees, particularly NALGO members, as a legitimate form of labour movement activity. Weinstein (1986, p. 41) concludes that 'the traditional positions of these trade unionists, although characterised as defensive, negative and obstructive by some Labour councillors, have actually stood the test of time rather better than the more ambitious hopes of their socialist employers'.

The 1989 NALGO National Strike

In 1989, for the first time in its history, NALGO took national strike action. This was seen by many activists as a qualitative step forward, a 'coming of age' as a trade union. The issue of the dispute was one which unified the NALGO membership, the defence of national conditions of service and national pay bargaining. The dispute took place in a context of rising industrial militancy in which there was also industrial action by rail workers and a relatively successful, albeit unpublicized, fight for the thirty-five-hour week in the engineering industry. The tactics adopted by NALGO in the strike were largely successful. These consisted of an escalating programme of national stoppages of one-day, two-day and three-day strikes and then selective strike action, with key workers withdrawn from work.

In the research on Sheffield NALGO a general question was asked near the end of the interviews about the effects the national strike action of summer 1989 had had on the branch. Most interviewees stressed the positive aspects of the action, namely increases in union membership, new activists coming forward, the recruitment of new shop stewards and a relatively favourable outcome. For instance, one of the leading shop stewards in Housing commented: 'We've had five new stewards come in as a result of the summer strike'.

In a number of cases shop stewards commented that they were surprised at the resolution shown by members who had not traditionally been active in the union. One of the union officers from the Education Department observed that the issue of keeping national negotiations on salaries and service conditions was seen as particularly important by the low-paid women workers in her department. She said:

> In the past when we've had disputes in this Authority that have affected the Education Department it's been quite difficult to persuade people to take any sort of action in support of other members. It wasn't difficult to persuade them this year that they should come out on strike. What really brought them out on strike was not the money but it was the strings attached, that was what brought them out. Their national negotiations, they still wanted to retain those and it proved to be quite easy to bring them out and to keep them out.... I think because they are badly paid and they can't see themselves getting any further forward, however hard you try, then other things become very important, and national negotiations I think they saw as a very important issue to them, because they do know that NALGO was trying however badly we do it to try and eradicate low pay, to try and move them up. And I think they thought any nationally agreed rates of pay are much more important than anything you can negotiate locally.

This quotation shows both the way in which traditionally non-active union members can become involved in a dispute, and also the way in which the issues of low pay and preserving national bargaining can be perceived as relevant by low-paid women workers. Defending national bargaining is not automatically thought of as a women's issue in trade union terms, but it clearly was in this case. Indeed another shop steward commented that the theme of defence of national bargaining was vital in achieving the majority for strike action. She said:

People recognized that the strike was primarily not about pay, it was about national conditions of service. My view is that if they balloted just on pay then people would have accepted the offer that was given on the first stage, but people voted against, people rejected the offer because of the strings that were attached to it.

In the case of the Land and Planning Department too, one of the shop stewards commented on the effectiveness of the action. This department was predominantly male in composition and had far more higher-graded posts than Education, but had perhaps comparable levels of union organization. He stated:

It was a milestone, people who had never even considered that they would ever be involved in a strike found themselves either out on strike or not in the office or even after the one-day action which everyone was involved with, they went on to the key workers who were out on strike. They'd come to work and find their colleagues in the next office had all disappeared and work was piling up and there were people coming round who had said 'Well look I voted no in the ballot, but it's great this, the whole place is dead'. The idea quite appealed to them, so it certainly faced people with the reality of what we're having to do in a way that was never the case before.

In this department key workers who processed planning applications were withdrawn, causing 'absolute chaos'.

There were, however, also observations concerning the loss to the union of some members who did not want to take industrial action, the relapse into inactivity of many members when the dispute was ended, and the limited nature of the victory. So while the overall assessments of the dispute were positive, they were far from unreflective or uncritical. Among the more critical observations, which tended to come from male interviewees, was the following:

During the dispute we had a massive response from every type of member we've got, I mean really wonderful. The atmosphere was brilliant. We could ask people to do anything. People took on jobs and didn't think twice about it, really extremely good, brilliant atmosphere. That no doubt contributed to the success of the outcome of the pay negotiations, but I suppose activists like me after it expected this to throw up new people and we'd be flooded with people to get on with things, and it's been the reverse. Although we've got some people who took on stewards' jobs and one or two new branch officers, it's been really flat. It's as though people have said to themselves 'Well we did a good job there, put a lot of effort in, but now I'm going away for a rest'.

This observation shows the difficulties trade unions face in sustaining high levels of membership activism outside the context of a major dispute, and the episodic nature of union involvement for many members. The following statement is even more cautious in assessing the gains of the dispute, arguing that it was largely a defensive struggle and that defeating an employer offensive is not in itself a victory for the trade union movement.

It wasn't a massive victory, a pay increase level with inflation and putting off the dismantling of national conditions; but that's not a great step forward, but as a defensive position it was a major achievement.

The interview material suggests that the dispute had a marked short-term effect on the branch, while the long-term effect, although positive in developing union activism, was more limited.

Forthcoming Merger

At the time of the interviews in 1989–90 there was considerable discussion among NALGO activists of the forthcoming merger among NALGO, NUPE and COHSE to form UNISON. Union mergers have been a major feature of the recent history of the trade union movement. The tendency towards mergers arises partly from changing patterns of employment, partly from a desire for economies of scale and partly from a desire for unity as a way of enhancing the bargaining position of trade unions. The problems of unions in the 1980s and 1990s have been well documented (McIlroy, 1988), covering areas such as loss of members, employer opposition and a difficult climate for collective bargaining. These problems at the time of the research in the late 1980s had not affected unions organizing in the public services to the same degree as unions in the private sector or in industries such as steel and coal-mining, largely because they had lost fewer members. Nonetheless public service unions faced problems arising from changes in the financing of public services, compulsory tendering, privatization and government opposition to national pay bargaining.

Much of the literature on trade union mergers (Buchanan, 1985; Undy *et al.*, 1985; Waddington, 1988) suggests that trade union mergers occur and work well if satisfactory career arrangements can be worked out for the full-time officials of the unions involved. Nonetheless union mergers also require affirmative votes of the memberships involved. Questions in interviews about the proposed merger elicited a range of responses. Some supported merger as a general step towards trade union unity, one informant even adopting an Industrial-Workers-of-the-World-type position, saying 'the fewer unions the better'. Some saw the removal of union divisions between blue-collar and white-collar workers as desirable and progressive, while some felt their members had little in common with members of COHSE and NUPE and that an enlarged union would have many internal conflicts of interest. Others were concerned about union democracy in a merged union, emphasizing their concern that lay officers should keep control over negotiations and not have full-time officials coming in and doing the negotiating for them. They felt this was an important tradition of NALGO not possessed by COHSE and NUPE which should be maintained. As one informant put it, 'What bothers me is the potential merger with NUPE and COHSE which are predominantly full-time officer dominated unions and that's something I feel very strongly against'.

In assessing these mixed responses to the prospect of union merger it should be remarked that they did not fall into any particular left/right cleavage or relate noticeably to any particular divisions of department, occupation or gender. The implications for women's representation in the new union were not mentioned by interviewees.

Changes in Employment Patterns in Sheffield

During the 1970s and 1980s employment in Sheffield, as in many northern industrial cities, was affected by the decline of manufacturing industry. The dominance of steel and engineering was reduced, with the closure of many small engineering factories and the loss of jobs in steel, especially following the steel strike of 1980. Jobs developed in the tertiary sector, in retail and leisure industries, although many of these were part-time jobs. The opening of the Meadowhall shopping complex on the outskirts of Sheffield in September 1990 was a notable example of this type of growth in employment.

At first public sector employment in local government seemed relatively immune to job losses. Sheffield City Council become increasingly important as the largest employer in the city. The city council had a 'no-redundancy' policy and a commitment to maintain levels of employment. During the latter part of the 1980s these commitments became increasingly difficult for the council to sustain, with legal requirements to put council services out to tender and reductions in local authority expenditure through rate-capping. By 1990 the difficulties in collecting the poll tax and government limits on council expenditure had produced a serious budget crisis and the council had to face the necessity of reducing expenditure on jobs and services.

These changes in the patterns of employment produced changes in the structure of the working population of Sheffield. An increasing proportion of workers were employed in white-collar and tertiary sector jobs. The social consequences of increased levels of unemployment became increasingly a matter of concern for local government, affecting the work of various council departments. The formation by the council of an Employment Department, later renamed the Department of Employment and Economic Development, to address issues of employment and job creation in the city, was an indication of these changes.

The council, and especially the Department of Employment and Economic Development, attempted to develop a number of partnerships with the private sector to create employment and economic regeneration. It decided to hold the World Student Games in Sheffield in 1991 and invested in a number of sports facilities. These projects encountered a substantial degree of criticism within both the Labour Party and the trade unions in Sheffield, partly over the issue of accountability of public money in partnership arrangements with the private sector, and partly over the desirability of expanding employment in leisure and retail sectors rather than in manufacturing. Traditionally Sheffield as a city, and its labour movement, had been built around the steel and engineering industries. Employment in these industries, while often arduous and hazardous, had been to a considerable degree skilled, permanent and highly unionized. While steel and engineering were predominantly male areas of employment, there were substantial numbers of women workers in these industries. Many of the newly created jobs in the retail and leisure industries were part-time and temporary, often required little or no training, and were frequently non-unionized. These jobs were typical of the types of predominantly female employment created during the late 1980s.

Changes in the Sheffield Labour Movement

The changes in the structure of employment in Sheffield had implications for the composition of the labour movement. In some areas of employment the jobs which developed were part-time and temporary jobs, the types of jobs unions have traditionally found difficult to organize. Membership of engineering and steel unions declined with the loss of jobs in these industries. Public sector and white-collar unions were seen by many union officials in these sectors as relatively immune from these changes. These changes could be identified in the delegate composition of the Sheffield Trades Council. The NALGO Sheffield Local Government Branch became the largest single delegation to the trades council.

Along with the changing composition of the labour movement went the decline of the traditional left, based on the Labour Group on the council, the Communist Party (which had long dominated the AEU District Committee), the Labour Party and the Co-operative Movement. This traditional left had long practised a form of socialist paternalism, with the Labour council carrying out socialist policies on behalf of the people of Sheffield, rather than mobilizing the population in support of those policies.

The collapse of the campaign against rate-capping in the mid 1980s meant that the council was forced to recognize that it could no longer carry out socialist policies in opposition to the central government and that it would, however reluctantly, have to impose cuts in jobs and services. Sheffield City Council increasingly looked to alliances with the private sector to provide employment and economic regeneration in the city. This orientation was the subject of much criticism within the Sheffield labour movement. This process led to a situation in which increasingly open conflicts developed between the council and its workforce. Weinstein (1986) discusses this process in relation to several Labour councils including Sheffield, although to define it in the Sheffield case as a collapse of a 'new left' would not be entirely accurate. This is because the Labour council, when led by David Blunkett from 1980 until 1987, was still based to a considerable extent on the 'old left' of the Labour Party and trade unions.

The Positive Action Research Project

One area in which the influence of 'new left' forces on the Council could be seen was in the area of initiatives concerning women's employment in the local authority. In 1984 a Positive Action Report was produced on council employment in Sheffield. The council established a one-year positive action research project following proposals from a Labour Party Policy Working Party on Employment. In Sheffield the District Labour Party (DLP) had set up various policy working parties to involve party members in writing the DLP manifesto for the local elections. Formally the Labour Group on the council considered itself accountable to the District Labour Party and often DLP meetings were held the evening before the Labour Group met to decide how councillors were to vote on particular issues. Socialist feminists in the Labour Party, who were also active in the Working Women's Charter Sub-committee of the Sheffield Trades Council, pushed the idea of a positive action project through the Policy Working Party in order to take forward the issue of positive action in council employment.

The Positive Action Report indicated that the local authority in 1984 had a workforce of approximately 32,000 employees of whom 7,500 were white-collar workers in APT&C (administrative, professional, technical and clerical) grades, and so eligible for NALGO membership. There was a closed shop agreement which required all council employees to join a trade union. The vast majority of white-collar staff were in NALGO, although a few opted to join APEX or MATSA, an action characterized by the NALGO shop stewards interviewed for this research as a way of being in a union without being in a union, i.e. they believed these individuals if they could choose would not be union members at all. The presence at the time of the research of a union membership agreement meant that all council employees had to belong to a trade union.

The 1984 Positive Action Report (Stone, 1984) found that the vast majority of the 4,500 women clerical workers were on scales 1–4, the four lowest grades for APT&C staff. This was the situation of 3,500 women, who comprised 80 per cent of the female APT&C workforce. The situation of women manual workers was even worse than that of white-collar workers, with cleaners particularly commenting that they felt stereotyped and stuck in low-paid, low-status cleaning jobs. Black women fared especially badly in council employment. There were very few black women working for the council and most of these were in unskilled manual jobs. Stone's research demonstrates the gulf between the Sheffield City Council's policy commitments to equal opportunities, with a comprehensive policy and code of practice on equal opportunities, adopted in 1981, and the reality of its employment structure.

Since the Positive Action Report was produced in 1984 a number of studies have been produced which have indicated the limitations of equal opportunities employment policies (Jewson and Mason, 1986; Webb and Liff, 1988; O'Donnell and Hall, 1988; Cockburn, 1989; Nelson, 1990; Aitkenhead and Liff, 1991), all of which recognize that the adoption of a formal equal opportunity appointment and promotion procedure does not necessarily produce any major changes in patterns of occupational segregation. Indeed, O'Donnell and Hall argue that wage policies aimed at narrowing pay differentials may do far more to improve the situation of the majority of women workers.

The History of the Sheffield NALGO Local Government Branch

The Sheffield NALGO Local Government Branch was a long-established NALGO branch, whose development has been influenced by the proximity of strong blue-collar union organization. Linn (1977) notices a similar influence in a study of NALGO branches in Glasgow and Coventry. One of the key indicators of the blue-collar influence was the adoption of a shop steward system. As the Sheffield branch service conditions officer put it:

> The shop steward system was actually introduced in the early seventies as a response by the branch at that time, to try and bring the union closer to the membership. Up until then only certain branch officers had the authority to negotiate with the council on a wide variety of issues ... members in those days had to go on a committee and argue at that committee that their grievance should be taken up by the union before it was actually pursued by the relevant branch officer, and people found that unacceptable and they found the union too remote from the membership, so they felt that what NALGO should adopt, and they pioneered it in Sheffield, was a shop steward system *which was by and large drawn from shop steward systems which existed in manual worker areas.* (emphasis added)

This statement shows that the adoption of a shop steward system was both the result of the influence of blue-collar unionism and a response to a perceived need to make the union less remote from the membership, i.e. to develop a form of union organization based more directly on membership activity. The main difference between the role of shop stewards and the role of the departmental representatives in the previous system was that shop stewards were intended to have a negotiating responsibility, so that negotiations and industrial action would be devolved from branch to departmental level. This change had been achieved with varying degrees of success in the different departmental shop stewards' committees. The NALGO shop stewards' committee in Family and Community Services was generally mentioned in interview, by both its supporters and its critics, as the best organized shop stewards' committee. One of its long-standing shop stewards described its working as follows:

I think the shop stewards system within F&CS works how the shop steward system is meant to work and therefore a lot of the responsibility is devolved to the shop stewards' committee.... When the shop steward system was originally introduced ... the idea was that the branch officers devolve responsibility for negotiations to shop stewards and shop stewards' committees. In F&CS we deal with all our negotiations ourself, and the branch is rarely brought in, occasionally for advice when we are taking things into the higher levels of procedures and occasionally if there are issues around shop stewards and mainly when the potential for industrial action is taking place.

The Sheffield NALGO branch was the first one to introduce a shop steward system, in 1974 (Nicholson, Ursell and Blyton, 1981). In 1977 the NALGO Annual Conference approved the establishment nationally of a shop steward system, but the implementation process was left largely to the branches (Ayland, 1980). In this sense Ayland contrasts it with the introduction of a shop steward system in NUPE, where the responsibility for introducing the system was given to the full-time officials.

The Nalgo Action Group, a left-wing pressure group within NALGO, had earlier campaigned for the introduction of the shop steward system. While its introduction in the Sheffield branch should not be put down to this influence, the branch was generally on the left within NALGO. It was a fairly radical branch and debates tended to be within the left, rather than between right and left. The branch executive officer explained the political differences in the branch as arising largely from different situations. Some departments were facing issues of enforced tendering and privatization and so had to engage in competitive tendering, while other departments were still waging more traditional anti-cuts campaigns. He summed it up as follows:

> It's differences on the left I would say . . . I mean given Shef-
> field branch you'd be hard-pressed to describe it as any other
> than a left-wing branch. . . . So on the issues in many other
> unions you'd have a battle with the right-wing, all that's took
> for granted in this branch, no one would oppose it.

One noticeable evidence of the radicalism of the Sheffield NALGO Local Government Branch was the presence of an international relations sub-committee. This sub-committee was responsible for organizing twinning arrangements with trade union branches in other countries and collecting for various international solidarity campaigns. In 1989 the branch also started organizing an international week, with speakers, exhibitions and a social evening, which became a successful annual event.

The political issues facing the branch in the late 1980s and early 1990s were concerned with the contradictions and crisis of municipal socialism. Increasing tensions and conflicts developed between the council and its workforce especially in the Departments of Housing and Family and Community Services. Weinstein's national analysis of these conflicts applies clearly to the case of Sheffield. Trade unionists were increasingly forced to confront political issues, such as rate-capping, the poll tax and the quality of services provided. This process was particularly acute in high-stress areas such as Housing and Family and Community Services, which had to deal with various aspects of the emerging social crisis. Political conflicts and dilemmas were also evidenced over various aspects of council employment policy, such as the move towards single status (the provision of common procedures and terms of employment for all council employees) which could be interpreted as an attack on white-collar trade unionism, if single status proposals involved equalizing conditions downwards. At times the council and its workforce were on the same side politically, for instance in the case of symbolic strikes against rate-capping, but at other times they were clearly in conflict.

The New Technology Dispute

One instance of the conflicts between the council and its employees arose around the introduction of new technology. In 1984 there was a major dispute, which involved extended strike action over a period of thirteen weeks, when the council attempted unilaterally to impose a new procedure for the introduction of new technology. Strike action was taken by a number of key workers, including staff in the Data Preparation section in the Treasury and staff in Housing and F&CS. The action culminated in a new agreement entitled 'Responding to Change' which introduced a number of procedures which NALGO subsequently found advantageous. Informants described the outcome of the dispute as follows:

> Basically we negotiated some of it in fine detail, although in essence they imposed it, and now they're regretting it, I think, because we use it and they don't like it very much.

> It imposes conditions on management that they don't like more than ones on us which we don't like.

As this statement shows, the dispute was not only about new technology, but about procedures regarding organizational change. There was an important gender dimension to the dispute, given the involvement of women workers in the use of new technology. The agreement produced substantial changes in the working situation of women workers in data preparation and ended the situation where any worker spent her whole day inputting data. Work had to be re-designed to provide workers with a variety of work assignments. The issue of working with new technology initially affected women workers most, but one of the female shop stewards from the Data Preparation Section of the Treasury Department indicated how these aspects of work were now affecting all workers, who were now coming to see the relevance of the dispute.

> There were staff in Treasury who didn't believe we should be out on strike, and there was a bit of bad feeling when we did go back to work, especially because we had this agreement for balanced work, and then Data Prep staff were going out into sections within Treasury and we were also getting like a half-hour tea break every two hours, things like this, and it didn't go down well with a lot of Treasury staff, but I think now that they are having to use the new technology they are learning to appreciate what we had to put up with years ago.

The agreement reached at the end of the dispute also brought other substantial benefits for women workers. For instance it included the right for all workers who were pregnant or thought they might be pregnant to withdraw from work with VDUs, which was a major gain for women workers in terms of health and safety. For some women shop stewards too the dispute involved a high level of involvement in union organizing and a rapid education in union work.

Rate-Capping and the Poll Tax

Spoor's work (1967) on the role of NALGO in creating the profession of local government officer shows the ideological commitment of NALGO to local government. Support for the principle of local government logically means support for mechanisms of raising public expenditure to finance local government, such as the right of the council to set rates or other local taxes without interference from central government. The issue of local government finance was both an economic and a political issue for NALGO members. Thus the Sheffield NALGO branch supported the council in campaigns against rate-capping to the extent of taking strike action when called upon by David Blunkett as Leader of the Council.

A degree of demoralization and cynicism followed the collapse of the campaign against rate-capping as Labour Councils moved towards setting balanced budgets which implied cuts and job losses. Some NALGO members felt that the council's redeployment processes worked out better for manual workers, who were sometimes redeployed into white-collar jobs. There were fears expressed in interviews of cuts in administrative jobs which were seen as non-essential compared with defending 'front-line' services. The practical outcome of this policy, however, was that some providers of 'front-line' services, such as social workers, ended up doing more of the administrative work and less direct work with clients.

The poll tax presented a much sharper threat to local government services and employment. It also produced more substantial political/departmental divisions within NALGO. These focused around attitudes towards non-payment and non-collection of the tax. NALGO members in the Treasury Department decided to implement the poll tax because they were faced with loss of jobs in the rates section, since work assessing and collecting rates would cease. One of the leading shop stewards in the Treasury Department explained their position as follows:

> Our shop stewards' committee is very unpopular in the branch because we have been representing our members and what

you have to remember is that we had a Rating Section that now doesn't exist any more and the members in there were obviously, if we hadn't introduced the poll tax, would have been without a job, and certainly there were three branch meetings called specifically to debate poll tax motions at which we had perhaps 250 of our 500 members attending in their own time, and only by that method did the branch agree to implement the poll tax.

In the Housing Department NALGO members were opposed to undertaking work in connection with the poll tax because they did not want to encounter the public opposition likely to arise from asking people questions about how many people were living in their house and what their relationship to each other was. Those involved in Housing Benefits and related areas also felt that to do this work would radically change their relationship with their clients, since much information received from clients had traditionally been treated as confidential. Thus representing the interests of their members and being accountable to their constituency led shop stewards in Housing on the one hand, and in the Treasury on the other, to adopt diametrically opposed points of view in relation to the poll tax. Such conflicts can be understood in terms of the size of the branch and the nature of the work in these very different departments, as well as political differences between the shop stewards in Housing and in Treasury. The account given by one of the leading shop stewards in Housing focuses on the trade union rather than the directly political reasons for their members' hostility towards the poll tax. She stated:

Well in terms of the poll tax work the Housing Department probably gets hit by it more than any other department. . . . The council has decided that the Housing Department are to collect it and to administer the rebates. I think the general feeling is summed up by the kinds of resolutions that get passed by the departmental staff, which are along the lines of they don't like the poll tax, they are opposed to it, but haven't enough confidence to fight it on direct political lines like that, but where anger starts flaring up like this half-day strike that we had a couple of weeks ago, where our service conditions and [job] descriptions start to be affected by the poll tax and because what was intended was to increase our workload phenomenally, not to put enough staff in, to expect us to grass on the claimants again were something that people working in the section are angry about because our job has always been one of treating people in confidentiality, and these were the driving reasons of the strike.

Conclusion

The debates about the introduction of the poll tax, the financial problems of local government and the provision of public services meant that shop stewards within the NALGO branch had to confront a number of political issues in their day-to-day union organizing. Many of these shop stewards, as social workers, housing benefit officers, and other providers of services to the public, also had to deal with these issues in their work. There were also major issues of employment policy concerning equal opportunities, the introduction of new technology, single status agreements and redeployment which the branch had to respond to. The Sheffield NALGO branch was operating in a city with strong Labour traditions, but with a decline in the traditional bastions of organized labour and in the funding for local government. All these factors presented the branch with a number of political challenges and created lively internal debates within the branch. The late 1980s were a difficult time for trade unions and for Labour councils. Despite the difficulties of the period, this study of Sheffield NALGO shows that trade unionism was surviving and indeed achieving some successes for the membership in terms of union organizing and negotiating.

Chapter 4

Shop Steward Activism and Occupational Position

Introduction

Much of the literature on union participation, as discussed in Chapter 2, explores reasons for union participation in terms of work-related factors, particularly commitment to work. This chapter first examines the occupational structure in local government as a background to research findings discussed in the second part of this chapter. For local government workers the issue of grading was important in terms of the rewards of work. Material in this section is organized under the following headings: patterns of occupational segregation; departmental variations in occupational structure and job grades; the grading system in local government; the history of equal pay in local government; regrading disputes; the issues of low pay and grading.

The second part of this chapter examines various aspects of the relationship between occupation and union activism drawing on data from the questionnaire and interview surveys of Sheffield NALGO. The detailed consideration of the influence of work on union activism is included in this book, in order to explore the extent to which women's and men's union participation needs to be explained in terms of work-related or gender role factors. This material is organized under the following headings: occupational distribution of shop stewards; occupation and attitudes to being a shop steward; occupation and bargaining priorities; occupation and industrial action; occupation and union facility agreements; occupation and shop steward turnover; occupation and women's representation within NALGO.

Two main conclusions stand out from both the questionnaire and interview research: the obstacles to union office-holding associated with inflexibility of work for lower-grade, chiefly female, staff (and it is noticeable that inflexibility appeared more of a problem than the sheer volume of work) and the motivators for union activism in terms of the work content of some departments, especially Family and Community Services and Housing, which seemed to encourage staff to develop their broader political and social awareness. This positive motivator for union activism operated for both sexes.

The Occupational Structure in Local Government

Patterns of Occupational Segregation

Local government is a field of employment which encompasses a wide variety of occupations. Many jobs on the white-collar side are traditional female occupations, e.g. secretarial and typing jobs, while others are traditional areas of male employment, e.g. surveying and accountancy. The 1984 Positive Action Report (Stone, 1984) on women's employment in Sheffield City Council demonstrates in its statistical profiles the consequences of this occupational segregation for men's and women's earnings. Men were more evenly distributed across the salary ranges, with their lowest representation on Scale 1–2, the lowest pay scale, whereas women tended to be concentrated on the lowest salary scales, with 56 per cent of female employees on Scales 1–2. At the other end of the salary scales, at Principal Officer level and above, were found 3 per cent of female white-collar employees and 25 per cent of male white-collar employees. The report notes that 'The proportion of men in each range increases steadily as the earnings level increases, and the proportion of women in each range decreases steadily as the earnings level increases' (Stone, 1984, Statistical Profiles, p. 3).

One of the case studies in the Positive Action Report examines the situation of women in the Data Preparation section of the Treasury Department, an exclusively female area of employment. This was a section centrally involved in the new technology dispute described in Chapter 3. An analysis of the staffing process revealed that only women were recruited to the data preparation jobs, which had few opportunities for career progression. Of a core workforce in the City Treasury, who were recruited as office juniors, some, chiefly men, went on to gain higher qualifications and promotion, while others, mainly women, tended to stay in clerical jobs at Grade 5 or below, which required no or lower level qualifications. The majority of professional accountants and computer specialists were men, reflecting the national labour force in such occupations.

This analysis highlights the importance of formal qualifications in the processes of recruitment and promotion. Women lost out in job terms both because they were recruited with lower qualifications, reflecting inequalities in the formal educational system, and because they were not given sufficient career counselling to take appropriate qualifications when in employment. While some women did have access to day-release they tended to take qualifications which reinforced their performance in their existing jobs rather than ones which would have allowed them to switch to jobs with more career opportunities.

The processes of inequality in occupation identified here are similar to those discussed by Crompton and Jones (1984) in 'Cohall', where local authority employment patterns tended to reproduce inequalities arising from education and training prior to entering employment. This can, of course, make inequalities appear 'fair' and thus harder to challenge. Thus at the level of organizational culture there is a 'fit' between the bureaucratic grading system and the use of formal qualifications for appointment and promotion.

Departmental Variations in Occupational Structure and Job Grades

The Positive Action Report (Stone, 1984) indicates not only the inequalities in grading between men and women in local government, but also the distribution of these inequalities by department. While women were concentrated on the lower salary ranges in all departments, there were some noticeable variations. In the predominantly female department of Education (Administration) 80 per cent of women were on the lowest two grades, Grades 1 and 2, in Libraries 79 per cent of women were on Grades 1 and 2, but in F&CS only 17 per cent of women were on these grades. Some departments (F&CS and Employment) did have a higher percentage of women on the higher grades and these may have acted as role models for other women.

The inequalities in men's and women's grading need to be explained in terms of the fact that the predominantly male departments tended to have more higher-graded posts, so that men worked in departments where promotion opportunities were greater. For instance one of the shop stewards in Land and Planning explained the relatively small numbers of low-paid workers in his department in terms of the occupational structure:

I think there are less [low-paid workers] than most, being a professional department, estate surveyors, building surveyors, transportation people, there's a high number of people working in professional jobs and that's where the bulk of the department's work is done. The admin staff are in a support role, whereas in other departments a lot of the basic work is actually done by admin staff because that is the nature of the work. (Shop steward in Land and Planning)

In the more gender-balanced department of the City Treasury the occupational structure was still one which gave men substantial promotion opportunities. One of the senior shop stewards in this department described it as follows:

In a normal department there's a pyramid structure where you have a lot of people on clerical grades and it peaks at Principal Officer level. Our department's more like an egg-timer where there's a large number of people on clerical grades, a large number of people on Principal Officer grades and relatively few in the middle. (Shop steward in Treasury)

These observations suggest that in studying occupational segregation by sex, it is important to look not only at the organization overall, but also to consider variations among departments. There was clearly more opportunity for promotion, because there was a greater proportion of higher-graded posts, in the male-dominated departments. These variations were also important for studying patterns of union activism.

A classification of departments by gender is provided in the Positive Action Report (Stone, 1984). This classification refers simply to numbers of men and women in departments and gives a three-way split as illustrated in table 4.1.

The Grading System in Local Government

Employment in local government is dominated by the grading system. The role of NALGO in establishing national pay grades for local government officers is explained by Spoor (1967). He argues in his history of NALGO that many reforms in local government were initiated by the employees, not the councillors. A 1918 NALGO conference motion called for a national salary scale for local government officers and this was achieved in 1920 with the establishment of a Whitley Council for local government, but not all local authorities paid according to the national scale. Indeed in 1940 only 553 of the 1,530 local authorities belonged to provincial Whitley Councils. In

Table 4.1:   Classification of Departments by Gender

Male-Dominated Departments
Works
Planning and Design
Environmental Health
Recreation
Cleansing

Balanced Departments
Estates
Housing
Museums
Treasury
Administration and Legal
Employment
Art Galleries

Female-Dominated Departments
Family and Community Services
Education (Administration)
Libraries

October 1943 a National Council was established with a national joint negotiating committee and in 1944 national salary scales were finally achieved, but without equal pay for women. The long campaign by NALGO for the establishment of national pay scales may have developed a union culture which was strongly committed to the defence of national bargaining and contributed to the readiness of NALGO members to defend it in the national dispute of 1989, when the employers proposed to remove many national agreements.

History of Equal Pay in Local Government

The 1932 Conference of NALGO debated the issue of equal pay, partly because some local authorities were substituting cheaper female workers for male workers. The 1936 Conference voted in favour of equal pay, but also voted to oppose the employment of married women in local government. In 1944 NALGO conducted a survey of its women members and found that 35,000 NALGO members (27 per cent) were female out of a total membership of 130,000 (Spoor, 1967). Of the women members, 75 per cent were employed in clerical work. In terms of equal pay the survey found that 6 per cent of women members were doing the same work as men and were receiving equal pay, 40 per cent were doing the same work as men and were receiving lower pay (on average around 70 per cent of the male rate) and 54 per cent of women members were doing work not normally done by men, so that no comparison of pay in terms of the rate for the job could be made.

This 1944 survey also found that 98 per cent of women members worked because they needed to support themselves, and 48 per cent were living with and partially supporting their parents. Sixty per cent of women local government officers were aged over 30. Given the presence between the war years of a marriage bar in local government it is, of course, not surprising that so many female local government officers were self-supporting.

A 1945 Royal Commission supported the introduction of equal pay into local government and the civil service but it took several more years of campaigning to achieve it. In 1945 the Whitley Council incorporated equal pay into national APT (Administrative, Professional and Technical) pay rates. In 1952 the London County Council granted equal pay to all its female local government officers and equal pay was achieved nationally in local government in 1955 (Spoor, 1967).

Thus NALGO was one of the unions which managed to achieve equal pay for its women members well in advance of the coming into force of the 1970 Equal Pay Act at the end of 1975. Equal pay was achieved in the context of a bureaucratic grading system, which may well be less sex discriminatory than performance-related pay or other payment systems found in the private sector, but which can place pay inequalities on a seemingly objective basis. Thus, given the formal presence of equal pay, equal pay issues for women in local government have tended to take the form of disputes over grading, in which issues of equal pay for women and better pay for low-paid workers are intertwined.

Regrading Disputes

Recently employers in local government have brought in performance-related pay for some senior officers in a move away from a bureaucratic grading system. In the Sheffield NALGO Local Government Branch, NALGO had not been involved directly with the negotiation of performance-related pay, which had been undertaken by a smaller union representing senior officers. The bureaucratic character of the grading system can be seen in the fact that interviewees reported that considerable time, sometimes periods of two years or more, had been spent on various regrading cases. Thus it could be argued that the bureaucratic structure of the payment system generated much work for local union officers.

Regrading claims were seen as a way of improving the situation of the lower-paid workers, and so the amount of time spent on them corresponded with the high ranking given by shop stewards to 'pay rises for the lower paid' in their priorities for collective bargaining.

One of the best known regrading cases the Sheffield NALGO Local Government Branch had taken up was regrading for the nursery nurses. This had taken three years of campaigning between 1985 and 1988, meetings in the House of Commons and industrial action. One of the leaders of this campaign described it as follows:

> Well I'd been a nursery nurse for fifteen years. I'd worked for the Education Authority for a long time, and in 1985 a group of us got together to try and do something about our salaries. At that time we were paid on under £5,000 a year, which sounds low now, but even then it was very, very low. We decided that we would get together to try and get in a regrading claim for nursery nurses and child care assistants (CCAs) in Sheffield. We set up a working party consisting of nursery nurses and CCAs and we had one of the branch service conditions officers to help us. We went through the local grievance procedure, collective dispute and in the end we got to the stage where the council was saying yes, we should be paid more money, but 'we haven't got any money to pay you'. And that was when we started the campaign and involved local groups, parents' groups. We got involved with governors, the governing bodies of schools and head-teachers and teaching unions, other unions who work in schools, such as NUT and the manual and craft unions. It was a long time, over a year, but in the end we did negotiate a settlement. We organized strike action, we were on strike for quite a while, we took selective strike action, and we'd just balloted for indefinite all-out strike action, when we actually got a settlement with the council. (Branch publicity officer, former nursery nurse shop steward)

This statement shows the lengthy nature of procedures in industrial relations in local government and also the political difficulties of negotiating with a Labour Council, which may concede the justice of workers' demands, but also claim inability to pay. The nursery nurses' campaign brought a number of workers into union activism who had not been highly involved before. It was thus an empowering experience for some of those involved, who had later gone on to hold branch office.

Following the achievement of regrading by the nursery nurses in the Education Department a similar regrading was obtained in a much shorter period of time by the nursery officers in F&CS.

> In fact way back when I was branch secretary, the service conditions officer started doing some work with the nursery nurses and the school clerks and as a consequence of that some three years later, with a very gradual schedule of industrial action, the nursery nurses in the Education Department secured a regrading. . . . It probably took them about three years to get from the point where they decided they wanted regrading to get their regrading. . . . Yet only this year [1989] the nursery officers in F&CS who are on different conditions, who don't get as many holidays and things like that and are on worse conditions than people in Education, with the people in Education, they decided they wanted actively to pursue a regrading claim. Within about four months from them deciding and from them withdrawing goodwill over certain things they thought were not in the job descriptions, they actually achieved a significant regrading, and they threatened industrial action and achieved it all within the space of four months. (Shop steward in F&CS)

Regrading had also been achieved, albeit with some difficulties in implementation, for forty technicians in Land and Planning.

> There has been one instance where we actually set the agenda, where we wanted the technicians regraded across the whole department, and that took two and a half years of solid work to actually get management to agree to the regrading. We got improvements for, I think it was, forty members of staff, who were amongst the lowest paid and doing more than basic work. People in that position do, in my opinion, work which is above what they're properly qualified or trained to do, so they're thrown in the deep end and they end up with more responsible work than perhaps they should have, and we wanted that to be recognized in this new scheme. (Shop steward in Land and Planning)

In the Education Department two of the school meals supervisors were pursuing an equal value case with the support of NALGO. This case shows clearly how issues of regrading were tied in with attempts to revalue areas of work traditionally done by women. One of the union officers involved in this case described it as follows:

Yes, it's myself and another school meals supervisor, who work in catering, which is a cinderella service anyway. It's a predominantly female service, so of course all the wages are depressed in that service, and there are all sorts of ideas floating around about catering, like if you can cook at home for four, then you can cook in a kitchen for four hundred. It's like people don't realise the skills that are needed for those sorts of jobs, and so for supervising, my own position, for supervising forty staff and five establishments, I'm paid a Scale 4, whereas a man in this authority for supervising the same number of staff and doing basically the same job as I'm doing is on SO 1/2. And so we decided as a constituency to take out an equal value case, and just two people are fronting that up, but it is a constituency decision, hopefully so we will get everybody regraded. We actually did win a regrading when we threatened to take it up, but they only pushed us up one grade, so we went ahead with the case.

We are at the point where an independent expert has been appointed and has done a job of work, the Local Authority then appointed their independent expert and NALGO's appointed their independent expert and we go back to the tribunal in January [1990]. (NALGO branch welfare officer and school meals supervisor, former chief shop steward in Education Department)

This statement clearly links the issues of job grading with sex discrimination in employment. The nursery nurses too felt that their work was under-valued because the vast majority of nursery nurses were female, although one of the nursery nurse shop stewards involved in their regrading campaign was a man, and a male service conditions officer had done much to encourage and assist their regrading campaign. Thus these regrading campaigns indicate responses by the union to the issues of both low pay and gender inequality.

Low Pay

The issue of low pay and regrading had been addressed in negotiations by a number of branch officers and shop stewards in the Sheffield NALGO Local Government Branch. There was a recognition of the importance of this issue especially for women members. A 'clerical career grade' had been introduced in the mid 1980s. Interviewees described this as follows:

> Well a lot of our clerks are paid on the clerical 1/2, that is in terms of money, but it's right at the bottom of the payment scale for local government workers, white-collar government workers, and the clerical career grade will take them up to Scale 3 or 4. So it's a way of actually coming in on a grade and knowing that over a number of years your salary will rise to, it's either Scale 3 or 4, instead of being stuck at the bottom for ever and a day, however much responsibility you take on in an office. (Female ex-shop steward in F&CS)

> I mean while we're still addressing all those issues of low pay we have been successful now in getting every member, except those who are new entrants, off Scale 1, so in APT&C they're on Scale 2/3 which is not massive in terms of the amount of additional money, but if you go to an authority like Rotherham, Barnsley, all those surrounding us, you will find their biggest single group of members are on Scale 1, and they're not just on Scale 1/2/3, you can progress, they're on Scale 1 and on it for life, unless they get a different job. (Executive officer)

The approach in the 'clerical career grade' strategy went beyond seeking a regrading for a specific group of staff in that it attempted to open up the grading structure to provide opportunities for career progression for all staff. For women workers especially, therefore, it provided prospects for job advancement, rather in the way that the 'Responding to Change' Agreement, which emerged at the end of the new technology dispute, had opened up job prospects for data preparation workers. At the time the research was conducted it was rather too early to determine whether these improvements in women's work situation were likely to lead to increased levels of union activism and union office-holding. Moreover it should be noted that the 'clerical career grade' did not necessarily provide opportunities for movement out of clerical work into the types of jobs which made union office-holding easier.

Occupation and Union Office-Holding

Occupational Distribution of Shop Stewards

Shop stewards and union officers who participated in the research worked in a wide range of occupations. They included several people in professional jobs, such as accountant, surveyor, architect, planner, librarian and social worker, and in a range of other fairly senior white-collar jobs, such as computer advisor and administrator, several technicians, and people in a wide range of clerical jobs such as housing benefits clerk and word-processor operator. The largest single occupational category identified was social worker (12.5 per cent of respondents).

Given the wide range of jobs and the absence of sufficient size-able groups in specific occupations for purposes of comparative analysis, much of the subsequent discussion of the occupational factor is organized around job grade. The interview data, however, do provide the material for the discussion of the relation between union activism and some particular occupations. The grouping of grades into three status groups is illustrated in table 4.2. The status classification of grades follows the work of Nicholson, Ursell and Blyton (1981) and Stone (1984).

The questionnaire data were analyzed using cross-tabulations to explore possible relationships between grade and aspects of union office-holding. A number of questions were asked to identify the pattern of union activism. These included membership and office-holding on departmental shop stewards' committees and the branch executive.

There were a number of posts available on most departmental shop stewards' committees, including chair, secretary and minutes secretary, but perhaps the most important post was chief shop steward. Under the existing union facilities agreement chief shop stewards were entitled to three days per week off work for union duties with cover. Of the ten informants (15.6 per cent) who were chief shop stewards one was on Grade 2, one on Grade 3, two on Grade 4, two on Grade 5, one on Grade 6 and three on Senior Officer 1/2. Thus holding of the important office of chief shop steward appeared not to be tied to any particular grades and indeed women seemed reasonably well represented in this office.

Table 4.2: *Informants Answering Questionnaire, by Occupational Status*

Low Status	
Scale 1	3
Scale 2	9
Nursery Nurse 1	2
Sub-total	14
Middle Status	
Scale 3	5
Scale 4	5
Scale 5	9
Scale 6	10
Sub-total	29
High Status	
Senior Officer 1/2	8
Principal Officer	3
Social Worker Scale 3	8
Social Worker Scale 6	1
Sub-total	20
Missing	1
Total	64

Those on higher grades were slightly more likely to be on the branch committee, supporting tentatively the general thesis that seniority in the job tends to support union activism. Thirty-one informants (48.4 per cent) were members of the branch committee, including two out of three stewards at Principal Officer grade, six out of eight stewards at Senior Officer grade, and seven out of ten stewards at Scale 6, whereas only eight out of seventeen stewards on Grades 1, 2 and 3 were on the branch committee. Those on higher grades also appeared rather more likely to hold posts on the branch committee. Of the eight stewards on Grades 1, 2 and 3 who were on the branch committee six (75 per cent) held office. Of the sixteen stewards on Grade 6, SO 1/2 and PO grades who were on the branch committee, twelve (86.7 per cent) held office.

Occupation and Attitudes to Being a Shop Steward

Informants were asked a number of questions in the questionnaire about their attitudes to being a shop steward. These included their views of what made someone a good steward and the good and bad things about being a shop steward. Informants were also asked how they became elected as a shop steward. In the interviews there was further opportunity to discuss the links between experiences of paid work and union activism. This allowed for the exploration of departmental work cultures and their relation to union involvement.

The majority of shop stewards had originally become union office-holders because they were asked to by their work colleagues (fifteen, 23.4 per cent) or were the only volunteer (nineteen, 29.7 per cent). The other most popular response related to interest in trade unionism (nineteen, 29.7 per cent). These findings support the general findings of research on shop stewards that a majority of union office-holders start off as reluctant representatives (Moore, 1980; Nicholson, 1976), although the degree of interest in trade unionism indicated should not be under-valued. When broken down by occupational status these figures still show a majority of reluctant representatives at all grades, although this is slightly less strong in the case of the higher grades.

Informants were given space on the questionnaire to write in their comments about what made a good shop steward. These responses fell into three distinct categories. Twelve stressed moral and personal qualities with statements such as:

Infinite patience and good humour.

Commonsense, irreverence, humility.

An ability to listen.

Eight stressed political awareness, with statements such as:

Active socialist.

Having a knowledge of local and national politics and economic policy.

Encouraging members to support other workers in dispute, and support for oppressed nations, e.g. South Africa, Palestine, to bring issues of disarmament and world peace to members.

Fifteen gave answers which emphasized competence as a union representative. These included statements such as:

Hold regular shop meetings. Good communicator.

To be able to communicate with management; to be able to negotiate a compromise; to make themselves available to members.

Ability to explain union decisions (with reasons) to members in ways they can understand (no jargon).

Represents the members' views and follows through the decisions taken at departmental meetings.

In terms of grade among the eight who emphasized political awareness and sense of internationalism, six were either social workers or on SO 1/2. This supports the 'educated radicalism' thesis mentioned by Nicholson and the arguments of Joyce, Corrigan and Hayes (1988).

The second set of questions about the role of the shop steward asked informants what they considered to be the good things and the bad things about being a shop steward. Grade appeared to have little influence on views about the good things about being a shop steward, but there was some connection between grade and views of the bad things about being a shop steward.

The one area where there appeared to be a noticeable difference by grade in relation to the good things about being a shop steward was in response to the statement 'I have learned a lot from being a shop steward'. Six low-status stewards put this statement first, as did eight middle-status stewards, but only three high-status stewards. Presumably higher-status stewards had more sources of other information about how the council worked. This learning aspect, almost a career development aspect, of union work was commented on by some interviewees. One (middle-status) shop steward explained how shop stewards learned about promotion opportunities:

I think probably people get promoted because they get to know more about the Poly, when they know the system better, they can see the opportunities as well. I think the average member of the Polytechnic doesn't see the structures as shop stewards see them as laying out on paper. You can read a departmental structure plan and not know all the background noise a steward has and so you know about opportunities, you know about vacancies before they arise. And because you know a lot more people you get a feeling for the person they need in that job and whether it's a good department to work for and so you tend to go for the jobs that you're going to get.

Another shop steward considered that her experiences as a shop steward when on a low grade as a data preparation operator had assisted her with college work, which she was undertaking in hopes of career development.

It helped me a lot with my college work, because it's surprising what you can learn, what I normally wouldn't have access to as well, because if I was doing a project on something at college, it would give me access to material that I would normally never see, and because I have been a shop steward, I've still got links with a lot of friends at branch office and I can still find out what is happening, so I still use these contacts for my college work and things like that.

There was more variation by grade in answers concerning the bad things about being a shop steward. Pressure from management was felt slightly more by staff on lower grades, although only a minority of informants put it first (9.4 per cent), second (9.4 per cent) or third (12.5 per cent). Those on higher grades especially tended to rank highly the response 'It creates difficulties in doing my job'. Those on higher grades also seemed more aware of conflicts with family and social life, with the four informants who ranked this factor first being on Grade 6 or above, as were four of the six who ranked it second.

The answers to these questions about the good and bad things about the role of the shop steward, when analyzed by grade, indicate possible differences in the relationship between job and union work for shop stewards at different levels of the organization. While low-status stewards found that union work gave access to information which they would not normally receive during their work, this was much less the case for higher-status stewards. For higher-status stewards there was more perceived conflict between job and union work, probably because the tasks associated with the job were more complicated and open-ended. This raises the issue of which jobs make it easier or more difficult to be a steward. This issue will be explored in sections dealing with the operation of union facility agreements and reasons for shop steward turnover.

In interviews, differences in work experience arising from the different organizational cultures in various departments emerged strongly. These clearly influenced union activism. The other important aspect, besides occupational status, of job-related factors affecting union activism is work content. Several interviewees suggested that the work in some departments, such as Housing and F&CS, was far more likely to encourage awareness of social issues, because the work involved dealing with clients who faced a number of social problems. Thus issues such as levels of public expenditure on welfare services and changes by the government in benefit regulations affected people's day-to-day working lives in the performance of their job. One welfare rights officer stated that when he started work several years ago his job was to obtain more money for his clients. Now his job more often involved trying to prevent benefits being reduced. These changes affected the stress level of the job, both because local government officers had repeatedly to learn new sets of regulations, and because these changes sometimes exacerbated the problems of the clients. It was thus impossible for staff in these departments to avoid becoming aware of certain political and social issues. Moreover the frequent contact with clients who were poor or in other ways socially disadvantaged led to greater awareness of social inequality.

> The other issue in F&CS is the levels of stress that people are working under. People feel stress more acutely, looking at all the poverty and social inequality in the world. People in there are inevitably going to be more aware of the fact that the world isn't fair, because they face it every day in their work. (Shop steward, ex-F&CS)

The work content meant that both the job and the working environment were stressful, which made employees more aware of the need for union representation. The social awareness of staff in departments like F&CS and Housing arose both because individuals who were interested in social problems were more likely to take work in these departments and because their work experience encouraged and deepened such awareness. Also, the professional training for jobs such as social worker involved acquaintance with social science material dealing with inequalities of class, ethnicity, gender and disability.

Observations in interviews recognized both the existence of distinct departmental cultures and the influence of this on the pattern of union organization.

> Nationally Housing and Social Services tend to be the most active departments. In Sheffield I would add Education Services. The job content makes people more aware of social issues.

Table 4.3: *Shop Stewards' Views of NALGO's Negotiating Priorities*

Negotiating Priority	Value of Ranking		
	First Ranking	Second Ranking	Third Ranking
Service conditions	23.4%	14.1%	15.6%
Higher pay	10.9%	17.2%	10.9%
Equal opportunities	6.3%	7.8%	7.8%
Shorter working week	3.1%	4.7%	7.8%
Health and safety	0.0%	12.5%	20.3%
More time off for trade union work	1.6%	0.0%	1.6%
New technology agreements	1.6%	1.6%	3.1%
Pay increases for the lower paid	35.9%	20.3%	9.4%
Job security	9.4%	10.9%	9.4%
More opportunities for training and promotion	3.1%	6.3%	6.3%
Workplace nursery	0.0%	1.6%	7.8%

It's the cultural atmosphere of departments. (NALGO branch organizer)

Occupation and Bargaining Priorities

Examining the possible relationship between occupation and bargaining priorities involves looking at how work experience and situation might lead to awareness of particular issues. This can take the form of responsiveness to the needs and wishes of the immediate constituency — and many stewards in their replies to questions about the role of the shop steward had stressed the representative rather than the leadership role — or it might reflect an ability to take a wider social and political view, which could be encouraged by working in occupations which particularly foster social awareness.

In the questionnaire study informants were asked to answer a ranked order question about bargaining priorities. In computer analysis these answers were broken down by gender, grade and department. In subsequent interviews questions were asked about perceived differences in bargaining priorities and their relation to factors such as gender, occupation/grade and department. Table 4.3 shows the overall answers to questions about bargaining priorities. The two most popular first priorities were 'pay increases for the lower paid' and 'service conditions'. 'Pay increases for the lower paid' may have been popular because it reflected NALGO's national campaigns against low pay in local government and also because it was seen as an equal opportunities issue. Thus it was to some extent, although not exclusively, seen as a women's issue, given the concentration of women members on the lower grades. Higher pay and job security, traditional trade union concerns, were also rated fairly highly.

In interpreting these results it is important to bear in mind that bargaining priorities reflect a number of factors. These include political and social attitudes, work experience and situation and also estimates of what the union can achieve and has achieved, for example an issue may no longer be a bargaining priority if the union is seen to have already achieved as much as it can in this field. This may well have been the case with 'new technology agreements', where a major agreement had been reached by the branch at the end of a dispute with the council. Answers to questions about bargaining priorities must therefore be interpreted in context.

Those on Senior Officer and Principal Officer grades tended to rank 'service conditions' and 'higher pay' as priorities 1 and 2. Pay rises for the lower paid (the most popular demand) attracted slightly stronger support among the lower grades, but five of the eight social workers put this first. Among the lowest-paid stewards, those on Grades 1, 2 and 3, thirteen (72.2 per cent) ranked this priority first or second. Grade had no discernible influence on other negotiating priorities.

Shop stewards in senior posts were aware of the need for higher pay for senior grades to recruit and retain staff in competition with the private sector, but they also often saw the need to improve the position of the lower paid, i.e. they expressed a sense of social obligation or trade union solidarity to those less well off; on the other hand those in less senior posts tended to see tackling low pay as a priority because of both their own experience and the demands of their constituents. Thus there were not sharp divisions among shop stewards over pay bargaining priorities, given these values and maybe also the presence of national bargaining on pay and conditions of service, which meant it was not a policy issue decided directly by the branch.

Occupation and Industrial Action

An examination of the relation between occupation and experiences of industrial action needs to consider issues of both militancy and opportunity to take industrial action. In the case of the higher-status workers there was no evidence that higher status led to more caution about taking industrial action, although this is often supposed to be

Table 4.4: *Experiences of Industrial Action as a Member of NALGO — All Shop Stewards*

Form of Industrial Action	Percentage Taking Part
Overtime ban	28.1
Work-to-rule	23.4
No cover of vacant posts	56.3
Ban on use of telephones	18.8
Refusal to take on new duties	35.9
Ban on talking to councillors	20.3
Ban on use of cars for work purposes	14.1
Half-day strike	50.0
One-day strike	60.9
Strike lasting under one week	6.3
Strike lasting one week to one month	1.6
Strike lasting one to three months	10.9
Strike lasting over three months	4.7

the case for white-collar employees. Indeed in one instance during the new technology dispute higher occupational status seemed to lead to a sense of obligation that higher-paid workers should come out on strike while lower-status workers stayed at work, since those on higher pay could afford it more easily, and this occurred in the Employment Department. This all took place within the framework of a union and political culture which to a degree treated industrial action as a legitimate activity for all employees.

The questions about experiences of industrial action in the questionnaire study were asked before the national NALGO strikes of summer 1989. These events led to all NALGO members in local government being called upon to take short strikes of one day, two days and three days per week in a programme of escalating strike action. The timing of the questionnaire study explains why some informants report no experience of industrial action. Fifty-three (82.8 per cent) had taken part in some form of industrial action as a member of NALGO.

The most frequently reported forms of industrial action, as shown in table 4.4, were no cover for vacant posts, and short strikes of half a day or one day. Some of these short strikes may have been symbolic, political protests in support of other groups of workers or over rate-capping of local government expenditure.

There appeared to be some connection between grade and experience of industrial action although this may be also a function of department. It has to be remembered that grade and department and gender are related in that those departments with more higher-grade posts have more male staff. Those on higher grades were more likely to have taken industrial action. This may partly be a result of longer periods of service. On Grades 1 and 2 only 50 per cent had taken industrial action, while all of those on Grades 3 and 4 had done so, as had a majority of those on Grades 5 and 6. All those on Senior Officer grade had taken industrial action, as had all the social workers and nursery nurses.

Some forms of industrial action had been taken particularly by selected grades and it is reasonable to suggest that this was related to work content and to seniority. The ban on use of telephones had been operated by all six field social workers and a minority of staff on Grades 3, 4, 5, 6 and Senior Officer level. Clearly the ban on the use of cars for work purposes could only be undertaken by those who used cars in the course of their work. The ban on talking to councillors had been carried out only by staff on Grade 5 and above and is obviously related to higher occupational grade, since servicing council committees and advising councillors is more likely to be a feature of work at this level. This is one of the clearest instances of a connection between grade and union activism, since it was a form of industrial action only operable by workers in particular work situations.

Occupation and Union Facility Agreements

One of the clear perceptions of interviewees was that it was easier to be a shop steward in some occupations than others. This related partly to flexibility and partly to other pressures of work, but especially to flexibility. At the time of the research NALGO shop stewards worked according to a union facilities agreement which allowed them to take time off as needed to do union work. On the surface this looked like a very good agreement from the point of view of the union, because it suggested that union representatives would be allowed to take as much time off as they needed to do their union work, but the problem with it was that there was no cover for the job the shop steward had vacated. This led to problems for stewards of work piling up and sometimes pressure from colleagues, managers and clients. In some jobs which were inflexible or involved supplying front-line services to the general public it was often difficult or impossible in practical terms to leave the job to do union work.

But is it difficult in some jobs for people to get time off?
Yet it is. If somebody works shifts in a children's home then they work with one other person for a shift. It can be difficult on a personal working relationship just to say 'I'm entitled to this time off and therefore I'm going to go'. There's no cover for people, which would be what would make it realistic, but there's no problem put in the way of someone leaving. The problem is of leaving colleagues unsupported and people don't feel able to do that, to walk off a small unit leaving work undone. It's not the same as if you've got paperwork that's not been done. You can do that a couple of hours later. If you're running a unit where you have to do something with kids or elderly people or in a day centre where you're working with mentally handicapped or people like that all the time, you can't just go off and leave them to go to a meeting and that does cause some difficulties sometimes. (Ex-shop steward, F&CS)

What this statement by a female ex-shop steward, who worked as a social worker at a day centre for mentally handicapped people, reveals is the contradiction between the formal union facilities agreement, which legitimated employees leaving their jobs to do union work, and the practical difficulties of implementing the agreement without cover. For workers in jobs which were inflexible, where they were dealing with clients whose needs had to be attended to instantly or continuously, leaving the job to do union work posed real problems of letting down their colleagues and leaving work situations which they often considered to be already under-staffed. Part of this problem, as the above statement indicates, lies in the perceived difference between jobs dealing with people and jobs dealing with paperwork. When looking at administrative jobs, however, the level of seniority is important. In more senior administrative jobs it appeared possible to reschedule and postpone work, but for more junior administrative and clerical workers, the problems of taking time off could be more acute than for professional workers. Another interviewee from F&CS described the problem as follows:

How well do union facilities agreements work?
It's very, very patchy, and it depends very much on the nature of the job that you do. Within F&CS, for example, someone who is not tied to a desk job all the time, someone who is

perhaps a field worker, case worker or something like that is more able to find the time to do the job of shop steward than people who are in administrative jobs, who find it more difficult. Because you take a typist away from the typing pool and it's typing that doesn't get done and it relies on other people doing that work. If I leave my office then my work will still need to be done when I get back there, although colleagues will support me by taking messages and things and perhaps the amount of work that I take on is less as a consequence. It is easier for me to do that than it is for a clerk or even, we've got a problem at the moment, for someone who is a home care organizer. She has a clear caseload and other people cannot absorb any of that caseload. For her to take time off to do trade union duties means the work doesn't get done. I think that sort of problem discourages some people who are in those sorts of admin jobs, and ironically it's the low-paid, often women workers. There is a sort of built-in discouragement for them to come forward as shop stewards. (Shop steward, F&CS)

The trade union facilities agreement worked rather differently in the case of chief shop stewards and branch officers, who had fixed amounts of times off, sometimes with another worker being put in to cover their jobs. Chief shop stewards had three days' facility time per week for union duties. Several interviewees discussed attempts by NALGO to negotiate more cover for shop stewards so that it would be easier for members to become union representatives.

We're involved in negotiations with management to try and ensure that it's not just time off but cover as well and that is for people who are in those types of jobs where it is difficult for them to get away to do trade union duties, because I think a lot of that reflects the sort of different levels of responsibility and the different number of issues that people take on. (Shop steward, F&CS)

A number of questions were asked in the questionnaire study about the operation of the union facilities agreement and the relationship between job and union work. These questions attempted to explore both how the job could assist union work and also where the conflicts might arise. In the interviews, the relation between job and union work was explored by asking whether in the interviewee's opinion there were particular jobs which made it difficult to become a union

Table 4.5: *Hours per Week Spent on NALGO Work — All Shop Stewards*

Number of Hours	Percentage of Shop Stewards
0–5 hours	31.3
6–10 hours	37.5
11–15 hours	10.9
16–20 hours	10.9
Over 20 hours	6.3

office-holder. A number of jobs were mentioned, such as residential social worker, departmental secretary, typist, nursery nurse, and bene-fits clerk. Generally the jobs mentioned as difficult to combine with union work possessed at least one of two characteristics: dealing with clients or the general public and being part of a 'front-line' service where it was hard physically to leave the job; or being in a lower-status administrative or clerical grade, where ability to carry out union work depended very much on the goodwill of work colleagues to cover the work of the absent ship steward. In these situations, the cover issue was clearly of crucial importance. The jobs were often, although not always, typically female jobs, such as nursery nurse and depart-mental secretary. The one job identified as difficult to combine with union office-holding which was likely to be held by both sexes was residential social worker.

In the questionnaire, informants were asked about the operation of the union facilities agreement and the relationship between their job and their union work. Firstly, informants were asked approximately how many hours per week they spent on NALGO work. The results are shown in table 4.5.

There was no clear connection between grade and hours spent on NALGO work in a typical week, except that six of the eight social workers spent eleven or more hours per week on NALGO work. So level of activism in the department may be more important, and of course time spent on union work will increase at specific times. The answers to this question did not reveal any substantial grade varia-tions, but the answers to questions about difficulties in taking off time for union work did.

Informants were asked whether they encountered any difficulties in taking the time off work for union duties which they were formally entitled to take. Twenty-one (32.8 per cent) answered that they did en-counter difficulties. These included the two residential social workers, three of the six field social workers, one of the two nursery nurses and

Table 4.6: *Sources of Difficulty in Taking Time Off for Union Work — All Shop Stewards*

Source of Difficulty	Value of Ranking		
	First Ranking	Second Ranking	Third Ranking
Pressure from managers	14.1%	3.1%	1.6%
Pressure from colleagues	1.6%	9.4%	6.3%
Pressure from service users	7.8%	4.7%	3.1%
Other factors	20.3%	3.1%	3.1%

a minority (around a third) of the other grades. Nonetheless this may have been an underestimate given other answers later in the question-naire and in interviews. The problem relates to the issue of the absence of cover. It appeared that many shop stewards were in a situation where no one in authority was explicitly challenging or impeding their operation of their rights to time off under the union facilities agreement, but there were still practical difficulties about taking time off. These difficulties were explored in the questions reported in table 4.6.

In write-in comments, twenty-two informants made references to pressure of work, either to do with inflexibility or volume of work piling up. This was not a factor arising directly from management pressure, but either arose from the work situation or from the stewards' commitment to their own work. Many of these comments referred to typical women's jobs, such as school secretary. Among these comments were:

> I am part-time and work alone — so I have not much time to spare and the work has to be done. (School clerical assistant)

> Being a residential social worker I often have to do trade union duties in my own time; it is then difficult to take time back because residential social work offers minimum staff cover. (Residential social worker)

> We may be short-staffed if both stewards attend a meeting. (Education benefits clerk)

> Consciousness of not getting work done myself. (Housing benefits officer)

> No cover. (Nursery nurse)

> Peaks of work load — immovable commitments. (Technician)

The problem of a backlog of work tended to increase slightly with grade, although a majority of all grades except Grade 2 identified it as a problem. Interviews showed that some were conscious of a backlog of work but did not let it bother them, while others tended to work late to cover all their work. Women seemed more likely than men to work late to make up work which they had missed because of union activity.

> *Is there a problem of work piling up?*
> The work does pile up, but I think the union's established a place for itself in this department [Land and Planning] and the management doesn't complain about it, or if they do never in a serious way.
> *Is that worrying for individuals though when work is piling up?*
> Oh yes, my desk's awash with work that's not been done. (laughter)
> *So how do you manage?*
> Well I mean, it just doesn't get done, you can only do what you can do, can't you. You spend a lot of time explaining to people why you're not doing their planning.
> *Some people have said they work late in the evenings.*
> No, no there's enough pressure during the daytime, and as far as I'm concerned anyway the evening's my own time. I don't donate it to the council. (Shop steward in Land and Planning)

On the other hand one ex-shop steward reported that as a social worker she did work into the evenings to carry out both her job and her union work.

> Well I was always pressed for time, but having said that you work flexible hour contracts, no one actually demands that you are at your desk from 9 to 5, it's quite easy to attend meetings and put off other things to later. It often meant I was working until 7 or 8 at night to attend to the demands of everything, so I suppose I worked, well if you think about only doing trade union duties in work time, I worked a lot of overtime, but I never regarded it that way. I always regarded it that I would do a lot of trade union work in my own time, which perhaps is not the strongest trade union point of view, but inevitably that ends up being the case for a lot of people. (Ex-shop steward in F&CS)

Table 4.7: *Times when Union Work Performed, by Occupational Status*

Time when Union Work Performed	Occupational Status		
	High Status	Middle Status	Low Status
Mostly in work time	60.0%	55.2%	28.6%
About half in work time and half in own time	35.0%	41.4%	50.0%
Mostly in own time	5.0%	3.4%	21.4%

In the questionnaire study informants were asked when they did their union work, whether mostly in work time, about half in work time and half in own time, or mostly in their own time. Thirty-two (50 per cent) said they carried out their union duties mostly in work time, twenty-seven (42.2 per cent) about half in work time and half in their own time, and for five (7.8 per cent) union work was mostly performed in their own time. These answers did show some relationship to grade, as indicated in table 4.7.

What these figures suggest is that the union facilities agreement tended to work better for those in higher grades, who had more control over their work and were therefore more able to do union work in work time. Of the five shop stewards who reported that they did union work mostly in their own time, two were on Grade 2, one on Nursery Nurse Grade I, one on Grade 6 and one on Principal Officer grade. Of the three informants on Grade 1, all did union work about half in work time and half in own time, as did the probation officer and the residential social worker and two of the three Principal Officer grade stewards. The groups in which a majority of stewards did union work mostly in work time (i.e. where facility agreements were working best) were Grades 3, 5, 6, Senior Officer and Social Worker.

Informants in the questionnaire study were asked two questions about the relation between job and union work. These were 'Does your job help you to be effective as a shop steward?' and 'Does your job conflict in any way with your work as a shop steward?'

These two aspects of the relationship between job and union work were separated out so that both sides could be examined. Tables 4.8 and 4.9 indicate the overall answers and then the breakdown by grade will be discussed.

Fifty-one stewards (79.7 per cent) said their jobs did help union work by allowing flexibility in the organization of work, but fifty-six (87.5 per cent) also said that inflexibility of work was a problem. It appears that these answers may relate to different situations and both indicate the importance of the job flexibility issue. Where aspects of

Table 4.8: *Job Support for Union Work — All Shop Stewards*

Form of Support	Yes	No
Giving access to useful information	60.9%	35.9%
Allowing easy access to members	78.1%	18.8%
Giving flexibility in organizing time and work	79.7%	17.2%
Helping develop skills useful in union work (e.g. public speaking, organizing meetings)	51.6%	45.3%
Giving access to senior management	56.3%	42.2%

Table 4.9: *Job Conflicts with Union Work — All Shop Stewards*

Form of Conflict	Yes	No
Conflict of time demands	78.1%	20.3%
Threat to promotion prospects	56.3%	32.8%
Problem of building up a backlog of work	62.5%	35.9%
Inflexibility of work	10.9%	87.5%
Conflict of responsibilities/loyalties (wearing two hats)	45.3%	54.7%

Table 4.10: *Access to Information from Job Useful for Union Work*

	Status of Shop Stewards		
	High Status	Middle Status	Low Status
Yes	70.0%	53.6%	30.8%
No	30.0%	46.4%	69.2%

work were flexible this was felt to be helpful with performance of union work, but where aspects of work were inflexible this constituted a problem.

Access to time flexibility at work increased a bit with seniority. Those on lower grades, especially the three informants on Scale 1, were more likely to report that their jobs did not help union work by allowing flexible use of time, whereas all those on Senior Officer and Principal Officer grades found their work flexible, as did all the social workers. Some questions produced a fairly even split between yes and no answers. In the case of 'access to useful information' the answers, not surprisingly, varied with grade. Those on higher grades were more likely to find their jobs assisted union work by giving access to useful information, as table 4.10 illustrates.

Table 4.11: *Conflict of Time Demands between Job and Union Work*

| | **Status of Shop Stewards** | | |
	High Status	Middle Status	Low Status
Yes	90.0%	86.2%	46.2%
No	10.0%	13.8%	53.8%

When looking at conflicts between job and union work a number of interesting differences by grade appear. We have noted earlier that problems of job inflexibility were experienced more by lower-status workers. The reverse side of this was that higher-status workers were more likely to experience conflicts of time demands, as table 4.11 shows, presumably because they had more autonomy in how they allocated their time.

The ability of the higher-status workers to do more of their union work in work time, i.e. to take more advantage of the union facilities agreement, meant that they were more likely to experience pressures at work because of conflicting demands on their time. No doubt this also reflected the more open-ended nature of their jobs. Overall the relation between grade and union work can be summarized by stating that lower-status stewards tended to suffer more from inflexibility of work, while higher-status stewards tended to suffer more from the problem of an accumulating backlog of work. For both groups the issue of cover was important to make the operation of agreements on union facility time more practicable.

Occupation and Shop Steward Turnover

An analysis of shop steward turnover rates was conducted by examining the branch list of shop stewards from 1983 to 1989. These lists supplied information which could be broken down by department and gender, but not by occupation/grade. The average length of service for stewards was two years.

In interviews, reasons for shop steward turnover were explored. Existing shop stewards were asked why they had decided to continue in office and ex-shop stewards were asked why they had resigned from union office-holding. In addition stewards were asked for their general perception of reasons for shop steward turnover.

Both 'positive' and 'negative' work-related reasons were given for resigning as a shop steward. In some cases stewards had ceased to hold office when they changed jobs or gained promotion.

What job are you doing currently?
I'm a team leader. That's when I stopped being a steward.
(Ex-shop steward, F&CS)

I think people tend to leave the shop stewards' committee
when they get another job. They feel that they have six months'
probationary service hanging over their head, so it's not a good
idea, it's not conducive to being a steward. So a lot say 'I'll get
in touch after six months' and never come back. (Shop steward, polytechnic)

In other cases informants in interview suggested that the reasons
for standing down as a steward arose from pressure from colleagues,
workloads and lack of cover. Thus the effective operation of facility
agreements may be more important in terms of stewards continuing in
office over a substantial period of time, than in terms of initial willingness to stand for office. In this sense good facility agreements are
important for trade unions as collective organizations. Unions need
some continuity in union office-holding to build up expertise, as well
as the election of new stewards to provide new energy and prevent
stewards getting out of touch with the members. There is also an
important principle of union democracy involved in that members
should choose whom they wish to represent them as shop stewards,
and this cannot be achieved if the design of some jobs makes it difficult or impossible for their incumbents to take on and continue in
union office-holding.

The following extract from an interview with one of the branch
officers who had formerly been a chief shop steward in the Education
Department illustrates these pressures. The Education Department
was a department with a large number of women workers, employed
predominantly on the lower grades.

How long do these shop stewards stay in office?
Not very long unfortunately. Usually about eighteen months
before we lose them, or if we don't lose them they cease to
function as an active shop steward. They're still there, but they
don't function as an active shop steward, and that's because
the pressures are placed on them because they tend to be in
secretarial positions, so no one covers their job if they go out
to do any trade union duties and it becomes peer pressure on
them, because they are leaving their work for somebody else
to pick up.

Occupation and Women's Representation within *NALGO*

Women's representation in NALGO will be discussed in more detail in Chapters 5 and 6. At this stage of the argument, however, it is useful to note that women were over-represented on the lower occupational grades in local government, as indicated earlier in this chapter, that workers on these grades were under-represented in union office-holding and that where workers on these grades did hold union office they experienced more problems of inflexibility of work and were less able to do union work in work time than their more senior colleagues. The problems of women workers in this situation are described in the following extract from an interview with an ex-shop steward. This illustrates the work-related barriers to taking on union office in the first place for many of these women workers.

> In my opinion the only people who regularly work hard and consistently in the department are the clerk-typists. Everyone else comes and goes as they see fit. That might be a reason why clerk-typists haven't got the time to be shop steward. . . . In the department at Senior Officer level and above, it's quite easy to say 'I haven't had time to do that, I've had meetings', sort of ethereal meetings all day and not have to account for where these meetings were, whom they were with, when they were, what was the purpose of them. Clerk-typists cannot just get up and walk out, because someone would say 'What are you doing?', but above them everyone just picks up a load of papers and walks out. (Male ex-shop steward)

The key issue indicated in this statement is the flexibility of work, although it also suggests a relationship between flexibility and ability to control the total overall workload.

Conclusion

In this chapter the occupational context of local government has been described to provide the necessary framework for analysis of the research findings. The social awareness that the content of work provided in some departments encouraged union activism for shop stewards. Occupational position and grade appeared to support union activism for workers in more senior positions, because of the greater flexibility of work, although they experienced more problems of a backlog of work than lower-status workers. For lower-status shop stewards, inflexibility of work constituted a major barrier to the effective operation of union facility agreements on time off for union work. Therefore this group particularly would benefit from cover being provided for shop stewards to do union work. Given the financial problems of local government at the time of the research (the late 1980s) and subsequently, such provision was unlikely to be achieved by the union in the foreseeable future. It is, however, reasonable to suggest that there is some connection between the under-representation of this group of workers as shop stewards and their difficulties, when they did become shop stewards, in taking time off for union work. This raises policy issues for unions about the way trade union facility agreements, while applying the same conditions to all employees, can work out more or less favourably for different groups of workers according to their occupation and grade.

Chapter 5

Gender and Union Office-Holding

Introduction

This chapter begins with a discussion of approaches to the study of gender differences in union office-holding. The main research findings concerning gender and union office-holding are presented in this chapter. The material is organized under the following headings: gender and distribution of shop stewards; shop stewards and childcare; gender and attitudes to work; gender and job status; the influence of departmental cultures; the election process for shop stewards; views of women's under-representation; 'careers' in the union; gender and attitudes to being a shop steward; gender and industrial action; gender and union facility agreements; gender and shop steward turnover; management harassment of female union officers and stewards; union activism and maintaining a personal life; women at branch officer level; NALGO's attempts to promote women's participation and representation in the union.

Approaches to the Study of Gender Differences in Union Office-Holding

Firstly, as discussed earlier, this issue raises the question of what exactly social scientists mean when they refer to gender differences. The term can refer to differences which occur along gender lines or differences which arise because of gender roles. As already argued, not all differences which occur along gender lines are necessarily the direct result of differences in gender roles; they may instead be the result of an occupational difference between men and women.

Secondly, when studying gender differences it is necessary to consider gender roles for both sexes (Feldberg and Glenn, 1979). It is not the case simply that women have a gender role which impacts upon their work and union participation, while men have an occupational role which is unaffected by their gender role. The male gender role in terms of union activism has, however, been relatively unresearched.

Thirdly, research should consider both gender differences and gender similarities. Writers on sex and gender differences, such as Oakley (1972), have noted that much research on sex and gender differences has focused on the issue of difference to the exclusion of similarity. This is particularly inappropriate in the area of union participation, since men and women may share many common work experiences which provide motives for union activism. As indicated in Chapter 2, there is an existing literature which addresses women's participation and representation, although the limitations of this material have already been noted, in that it is better at explaining barriers to participation than motives for participation. Moreover it has often started out from an assumption of gender difference, namely an uncritical acceptance of the common belief that women are less active in unions than men, thus overestimating men's levels of union activism.

It is important to look at both gender differences and gender similarities. This is a major issue in feminist theory both methodologically and politically. The area of women's situation in trade unions is a useful one for examining these issues, because of the nature of trade unions as collective organizations. There are problems for unions in recognizing diversity of membership interests, since unions are formed on the recognition of common interests of workers; nonetheless, more politically sophisticated approaches to trade union unity recognize the existence of membership heterogeneity and accept that structures and policies have to be organized to take account of a diversity of membership interests, including those which occur on the basis of gender. The question, however, is how far male and female workers have different material interests.

Feminist perspectives which have influenced trade unions in recent years offer a variety of answers to this question. From the radical and revolutionary feminist view, trade union unity is logically impossible since men are seen as not merely the agents but the cause of women's oppression. Patriarchy theorists, who identify patriarchy as 'the main enemy', also advance an analysis which makes trade union unity difficult. For socialist feminists (Cockburn, 1983; Hartmann, 1979) who identify a twofold struggle against capitalism and patriarchy, feminist participation in the trade unions is seen as worthwhile. Their belief, however, in the existence of two modes of production, capitalism and patriarchy (following the analysis of Delphy (1984)), means that trade union unity is inevitably problematic. Recently some socialist feminists

Table 5.1: Shop Stewards Answering the Questionnaire, by Occupational Status and Gender

Occupational Status	Gender		
	Male	Female	Total
High Status	18 (90.0%)	2 (10.0%)	20 (100%)
Middle Status	20 (69.0%)	9 (31.0%)	29 (100%)
Low Status	3 (21.4%)	11 (78.6%)	14 (100%)

Table 5.2: Interviewees by Occupational Status and Gender

Occupational Status	Gender		
	Male	Female	Total
High Status	7 (63.6%)	4 (36.4%)	11 (100%)
Middle Status	4 (50.0%)	4 (50.0%)	8 (100%)
Low Status	0 (0.0%)	3 (100%)	3 (100%)

such as German (1989) have challenged the belief in the existence of two modes of production, arguing that the dominant mode of production is capitalist. This approach makes the question of trade union unity less problematic, because it does not assert that male workers have any material interest in the continued oppression of women.

Gender and Distribution of Shop Stewards

Given the relationship already argued between work experience and union activism, this account will first summarize some general descriptive material about the work of male and female union activists, before going on to analyze patterns of union office-holding. This will include a discussion of sources of union activism, in terms of barriers to and enablers of women's union activism and the departments where women shop stewards came from. Table 5.1 indicates the occupational status of the shop stewards who answered the questionnaire. Table 5.2 gives similar data for the interviewees. The pattern of gender inequality in occupational grade reflects the gender inequalities in local government employment (Rees, 1990).

Table 5.3: *Annual Numbers of Male and Female Shop Stewards in the Sheffield NALGO Local Government Branch*

Year	Male	Female
1983/4	106 (68%)	49 (32%)
1984/5	99 (57%)	75 (43%)
1985/6	109 (60%)	73 (40%)
1986/7	118 (63%)	69 (37%)
1987/8	136 (71%)	55 (29%)
1988/9	104 (75%)	35 (25%)
1989/90	85 (67%)	42 (33%)

The questionnaire survey in 1987–89 was answered by forty-two male and twenty-two female stewards. This gave a slight over-representation of the proportion of female stewards by comparison with the branch records for that time. Study of the annual lists of shop stewards for the years 1983 to 1989 gave the overall distribution of male and female stewards shown in table 5.3.

There are a number of possible reasons for the general under-representation of women as shop stewards in proportion to their number among NALGO members, which was slightly over 50 per cent in the Sheffield NALGO branch. These include childcare, job status, shop steward recruitment processes and gender role.

Shop Stewards and Childcare

From biographical data supplied by the shop stewards answering the questionnaire there was a noticeable absence of mothers, but not fathers, of young children among shop stewards. For women it appeared that childcare responsibilities, as well as paid work, were difficult to combine with union office, but in interpreting this it is necessary to remember that many women with young children are out of employment altogether, and hence out of the trade union movement (Martin and Roberts, 1984; Rees, 1990).

Table 5.4: *Presence of Children among Shop Stewards, by Gender of Shop Steward*

Gender of Shop Steward	Presence of Children	
	YES	NO
Male	25 (60%)	17 (40%)
Female	8 (36%)	14 (64%)
Total	33 (52%)	31 (48%)

Table 5.5: *Age of Youngest Child of Shop Stewards, by Gender of Shop Steward*

Age of Youngest Child	Gender of Shop Steward		
	Male	Female	Total
Under 5	9	0	9
5–11	6	1	7
11–14	2	0	2
14–18	2	1	3
over 18	5	6	11
No children	18	14	32
Total	42	22	64

Slightly over half of the shop stewards had children, with a majority of the male stewards (60 per cent) having children, while a majority (64 per cent) of the female stewards did not have children. This pattern fits with other research on female union office-holders reported in Chapter 2. The gender differences were greater when the age of children was considered. None of the female stewards had a child under 5, whereas nine of the forty-two male stewards did. Of the eight female stewards who had children, in six cases all the children were over 18.

Table 5.5 suggests that male stewards found it easier to combine parental responsibilities with union office-holding than female stewards did, reflecting an unequal division of labour within the home and the exclusion of many mothers of young children from employment. The issue of childcare was commented on by some interviewees as a factor which restricted union participation. For some members it prevented their becoming shop stewards. For some shop stewards it was seen as a factor which prevented their becoming branch officers, because of the number of evening meetings involved.

Childcare is a critical issue for shop stewards, especially those with young children. There are problems of working late to do work and make up time. (Female branch officer)

Many shop stewards have no children or grown-up children. There are creche arrangements at union meetings or the payment of babysitting expenses. (Male branch organizer)

If I think about it most women who are active in NALGO, most of them haven't got kids or have got grown-up kids. (Chief shop steward)

Do you think women have any particular difficulties being active in the union?
Yes I think if they've got commitments at home, childcare problems, some of the meetings are after school time. It can be difficult for them to take an active part if they're a one-parent family and haven't got anyone to take care of the children. (Female ex-shop steward)

How do you find being a parent and being a shop steward?
Well I must admit I have tended not to go to as many evening meetings as I would have liked to have done. The executive's every fortnight on a Thursday, and I must confess the number of times I went to that were very limited, just because of the fact that I needed to get home, because my wife had been home all day. My going to evening meetings just wasn't fair on her. By five o'clock she was ready to go and have a rest. (Male shop steward)

How do you cope being a single parent and a shop steward?
It can be tricky sometimes, like last week when it was half-term holiday. I was off work, but the Joint Consultative Committee and the recognition issue was on, so I spent Monday basically running around town with two kiddies in tow. I don't see it as a particular problem. I've got that side fairly well sewn up. It can be difficult sometimes when we're in negotiations. I might be late home, but that's more hitting me in the pocket than any problems with kids. I don't think that I could stand as a branch officer at the moment in the situation I'm in. When I was a branch officer I was negotiating until after midnight and I couldn't leave the kids with the childminder till after

midnight, so it does limit me from that point of view. But on my role in the department it has no effect. (Male shop steward, ex-branch officer)

Your children are all grown-up. Could you be a branch officer if you had young children?
No, no, it would be impossible. (Female branch officer)

These observations suggest that childcare responsibilities affected the union activism of both male and female shop stewards, but to different degrees. Childcare responsibilities certainly restricted men's union activity, particularly at branch officer level, but they did not imply a complete end to union activism, as appeared to be the case for some women members.

Gender and Attitudes to Work

In the questionnaire study, informants were asked a number of questions about their attitude to their job. Overall the replies demonstrated a high level of commitment to work. Some answers did indicate a gender difference, in terms of different replies from men and women. Proportionately more women (18 per cent) than men (12 per cent) agreed with the statement 'my job is dull and repetitive', but it was only a minority for both sexes. More women (100 per cent) than men (78 per cent) agreed with the statement 'I am capable of doing more responsible work than my job allows', suggesting that both sexes felt under-utilized at work, but women especially so. In response to the statement 'my job allows me to develop my abilities', 45 per cent of the women and 57 per cent of the men agreed. These replies suggest that women experienced a somewhat poorer quality of working life than men.

Also, more women (77 per cent) than men (62 per cent) agreed with the statement that 'my job is socially useful and worthwhile'. This may reflect the greater employment of women in 'caring' jobs or it may be a perception of work arising from gender roles. On some other questions about attitudes to work there was no or minimal gender difference. Workers of both sexes found their jobs interesting and varied, believed that they had too much work to do and rejected a purely instrumental orientation to work. While these questions produced some interesting gender differences, which fit with the occupational patterns in the City Council, they also show substantial similarities between women and men in attitudes to work. In short, the majority of shop stewards of both sexes demonstrated a commitment to work, which many writers on industrial relations have identified as a motivator of union activism.

Gender and Job Status

Another factor mentioned by some interviewees to explain the under-representation of women as shop stewards was job status. This was often linked with confidence and the ability to control one's work situation to fit in union work.

> *Why do you think women are under-represented as shop stewards?*
> Well men tend to be higher up, have more experience of meetings, sitting on committees and have more confidence. So more men get to be shop stewards. They're more confident.

As already discussed in Chapter 4, union facility agreements worked less well for stewards in lower-status jobs because of the inflexibility of work. Given the concentration of women in these jobs, this made union office-holding difficult for many women workers. A female ex-shop steward described these job-related problems in relation to her past jobs as a data preparation officer and a desk clerk in the Rates Hall and her current more senior administrative post.

> There was no flexibility in Data Prep. There were deadlines to be met. The work had to be done by a certain date. It couldn't be left. When I moved out of Data Prep I went to work on the cash counter. There was a majority of women there. I did feel guilty if I had to go to a meeting and the Rates Office was packed out, taking twenty minutes for people to get through the queue to pay their rates, and everyone was really busy, and I'd feel guilty about having to go to a meeting. You know one person's not going to make any difference but I still felt guilty.
> The job I'm in now, if I was a shop steward, I could do things like reschedule work. I know I've got a meeting next week and it's going to last all afternoon, so I'll have to work that bit harder the day before to make sure I get that work done or I can leave it till the next day and do it. (Female ex-shop steward)

This account combines work-related factors and possibly aspects of the feminine gender role. It shows how inflexibility of work in low-status jobs made it harder to take time off for union work, but also how the informant felt 'guilty' for leaving the job. Also she indicates her intention to cope with the meeting next week by making up the work she should do then either the day before or the day after. She does not suggest that she might cancel or defer it, a response which a number of male informants gave. In interviews it tended to be the women who talked about working late or taking work home to make up work missed because of union activity. It is possible that this reflects more conscientiousness about work on the part of women or less assertiveness about their right to time off for union work. This point will be explored further in discussion of the operation of union facility agreements later in this chapter.

The Influence of Departmental Cultures

It was noticeable that women shop stewards tended to come particularly from some departments. The likelihood of a department producing a substantial number of women shop stewards depended partly on the number of women in the department and partly upon their level of seniority. In the study of Sheffield NALGO the only department with a majority of female stewards anwering the questionnaire was Education (twelve, 70.6 per cent), which was one of the departments where the majority of the workforce was female. It has been suggested that women are more likely to take on union leadership roles when women are in a majority (Cobble, 1990; Wertheimer and Nelson, 1975). Wertheimer and Nelson, for example, write: 'The evidence is that where women constitute a large proportion of union membership, their participation is judged to be higher than where they are heavily outnumbered' (p. 26).

One of the branch officers in interview remarked that many leading women branch activists had come from Family and Community Services. If women activists come disproportionately from female-dominated departments, then this may be evidence of personal-societal-cultural factors affecting union participation. The departmental culture may also be relevant. A study of the branch records of annual lists of shop stewards allowed some more consideration of the relation between gender balance in the department and women's union office-holding.

The annual lists of shop stewards for the Education Department, the department with the largest number and highest proportion of women workers, showed that the balance of male and female stewards changed from year to year. In some years there was a majority of female stewards, in some a majority of male stewards. Thus while the gender proportion factor may have contributed to bringing more women forward to take on union office, this factor did not produce a majority of women every year. In the female-dominated department of F&CS women stewards were in a minority in each year surveyed.

Nonetheless, when both of these departments are compared with some of the gender-balanced or male-dominated departments they still did produce more women representatives and the gender inequalities in representation were not so sharp. For instance the gender-balanced department of the City Treasury showed a continuing and often marked under-representation of women as stewards, while in Works there were no women shop stewards in most years.

In interviews, two branch officers (one male and one female) noted how women branch officers tended to come from departments such as F&CS and Housing. This was explained in terms not only of the number of women in these departments, but also of the number of women in senior posts in these departments. In short, they were arguing that women's occupation of a leadership role was accepted within the departmental culture. Wertheimer and Nelson note that women are more likely to be interested in union work and willing to take on office when they see themselves as having prospects of advancement at work (Wertheimer and Nelson, 1975, p. 118). They also discuss the importance of role models to encourage women's union participation, a factor remarked upon by some interviewees. It is likely that the role model factor for many women office-holders was important initially at the departmental level, since this was the level where most activists gained experience of union work before proceeding to hold a post on the branch committee.

Departmental cultures may contain not only norms about the acceptability of women taking on leadership posts and positions of responsibility, but also attitudes towards gender roles in the wider society. In departments in which there was a strong commitment to equal opportunities and a degree of acceptance of feminism, it may have been easier for women to become active trade unionists. Women in such departments would not be constrained by a cult of femininity in which union activism or militancy was seen as unfeminine. It is likely that women in more 'radical' departments, such as F&CS, were more likely to receive support for union activism than women in departments like Education, where attitudes towards gender roles were rather more traditional.

Another aspect of the departmental union culture which affected female representation was the degree of support provided by departmental shop stewards' committees for the induction and training of new stewards. While this is of great help to all stewards, women particularly may benefit, if they are likely to be held back from taking union office because of lack of confidence in their abilities, a trend noted by Wertheimer and Nelson among their personal-societal-cultural barriers to participation. For instance one female branch officer, who had been a shop steward in F&CS, described the help the system of support there gave to new stewards.

> F&CS has got to be one of the best organized departments in the branch. They have a very active shop stewards' committee. It's very supportive to new shop stewards. The shop stewards' committee always has an introduction day for new shop stewards to introduce them to the current issues in the department. It's a reasonably large department and they pair up new and experienced stewards to work together, so that the new stewards can learn from others' experience. I think for me the advantage of starting as a shop steward in a department like that was that you were able to get support. I am sure that people who come through that shop steward system are more confident and more able in a lot of ways.

This statement illustrates the importance of union-related factors in encouraging women's participation.

The Election Process for Shop Stewards

A third factor identified from the research findings which may contribute towards explaining the under-representation of female shop stewards was the process of selection of shop stewards. In the questionnaire survey informants were asked a rank order question about how they became a shop steward in the first place. Some responses, such as being interested in trade unionism or being the only volunteer prepared to do the job, showed minimal gender difference, but men appeared to be more likely than women to be asked to be shop stewards, as table 5.6 illustrates.

This suggests that there may be a gender difference in the path to union office-holding, which arises not from the attitudes of female shop stewards themselves, but from the attitudes of their work

Table 5.6: Shop Stewards Asked to Stand for Election by Work Colleagues

Value of Ranking	Gender	
	Male	Female
First Ranking	31.0%	9.1%
Second Ranking	35.7%	22.7%
Third Ranking	14.3%	27.3%

colleagues, who may be less likely to look to women to take on leadership roles. Given that many shop stewards start off as reluctant representatives, who are initially pushed into union office-holding by others, this may be an important factor in explaining women's under-representation in union office-holding. This is especially the case in NALGO, given that holding the office of shop steward was usually the key to more senior union office-holding.

Views of Women's Under-Representation

Possible reasons for women's under-representation in union office-holding were explored in a number of interviews. Explanations of women's under-representation were given which focused both on gender role attributes and job-related factors. These particularly focused on confidence and political awareness, although their links to low occupational status and lack of trade union skills and expertise can be seen.

One of the female shop stewards gave an account of the nursery nurses' regrading campaign, which stressed the lack of confidence that women in low-status jobs often experienced. The nursery nurses had been able to get organized with the help of a male service conditions officer, who recognized their difficulties and helped support their self-organization.

> About fifteen years ago, a group of nursery nurses came along to say that we were under-paid and under-valued and we were told at that time that we had to get ourselves organized, but that was easier said than done. So we went away, but we didn't know which way to go forward. About four years ago we decided to take up the issue again. We had a very good service conditions officer, who said 'Yes you've got to get yourselves organized, but I'll help you get yourselves organized'. It's

different someone saying 'You go and do it' without giving
you any positive advice, but to actually be with you and say
'Right I'll show you how to do it' made the whole thing different. He gave us the positive image of saying 'You're the
nursery nurses, you know what you're fighting for and when
we go into meetings you put the point of view'. Although at
the time I thought I could not do it, I went in and did it and
it did prove to be the right way. It's having that confidence to
go and face committee members and councillors and have that
confidence to speak, which I think basically women don't have.
They always tend to take a back seat and think somebody else
can do it. I still do that at times. I'm aware that I do it and I
try to overcome that and think no I must go forward and say
something.

What is noticeable about this account is not only the identification of the problem as a lack of confidence on the part of women, but
also a clear ability to distinguish from experience between right and
wrong ways for branch officers to organize members. Trade union
organizing is in many ways a learned skill. Whereas simply telling the
nursery nurses to get on with getting themselves organized had proved
ineffective, where there had been an attempt to share union organizing
skills and empower women this had proved more successful.

Another informant from the Education Department, which was
one of the departments with many women workers on low grades, discussed the problems of female union representation in the department
in these terms:

Are there mainly women workers in Education?
Predominantly women. The service I work in is a totally female service and obviously all the women are in the lower-
paid sections of the Education Department.
*Is it particularly difficult to organize that group and to get them
to stand as shop stewards?*
Very difficult, because they're not politicized at all and for all
sorts of reasons. Difficult to get women to stand as shop stewards and the reason women stand as shop stewards is invari-
ably because they have had some sort of personal grievance
and they come to trade unionism through dealing with that
and eventually stand as a shop steward. (Female branch officer,
ex-chief shop steward)

This account identifies both the low status of the women workers and their non-politicized culture. Where women did stand as shop stewards this was often seen as the result of a particular issue or grievance. Sometimes when this issue had been resolved the motivation to stay as a shop steward declined, especially if there was pressure of work or pressure from work colleagues about taking time off for union work. The interview stage of the research identified two female ex-shop stewards from other departments than Education who had also become shop stewards over specific issues and then resigned after a year or two.

In the Housing Department at the time of the research the ratio of male to female stewards was three to one, although slightly over half of the membership in the department was female. One of the female shop stewards discussed this under-representation in the following terms:

> It's something that exists right the way across the board and the first obvious reason is because of the way society works against women, because society is not equal. ... I'm not just talking about trade unions now, I'm talking about society in general, because sexism exists, because women's oppression exists. I think that that's why you always see fewer women coming forward. (Female shop steward)

What is interesting about this answer is the way the problem is located at the level of society. It is also noteworthy that at the time of the research there was this under-representation of women in Housing, because Housing (along with F&CS) was one of the departments with more senior women local government officers. Housing and F&CS tended to be seen by the branch officers not only as activist departments, but as departments from which women shop stewards and branch officers were likely to come.

'Careers' in the Union

Women's representation at the shop steward level is important because holding the office of shop steward is often, at least at the start of a union career, the first stage for further union office-holding. In the questionnaire survey, questions were asked about participation in a number of branch and departmental committees. Twelve women (54.5 per cent) and fifteen men (35.7 per cent) held posts of responsibility on their departmental shop stewards' committee.

Five male and five female chief shop stewards answered the questionnaire. The annual lists of shop stewards for 1983–89 indicated twenty-six male and thirteen female chief shop stewards during this period, which was proportionate to the number of male and female shop stewards in the branch. Other posts of responsibility on the departmental shop stewards' committee included chair, secretary and minutes secretary.

What these figures suggest is that once women became shop stewards they did not seem to encounter any particular barriers or discrimination in taking on posts on the departmental shop stewards' committee. This may indicate that when researching women's levels of participation and representation in unions, it is important to be specific about the particular level of the union structure under discussion, since different barriers may be present or absent at different levels.

Given the presence of possibly around 200 stewards in the branch, not all stewards were necessarily members of the branch committee, although this practice varied from department to department, as did levels of attendance at the branch committee. Nine female and twenty-two male stewards (respectively 40.9 per cent and 52.4 per cent of the sample) were members of the branch committee. This represents a degree of female under-representation at this level, which may be partly related to the timing of meetings, which were held in the evening. In interview, however, some informants did indicate that shop stewards from their department did not go to the branch committee often because they did not find it a useful union structure. So there are departmental as well as gender role factors involved here.

So women were under-represented as shop stewards and as members of the branch committee. Within the ranks of shop stewards they were not under-represented proportionately as chief shop stewards or in other posts on departmental shop stewards' committees. Once women were members of the branch committee they did not appear to be under-represented in office-holding on the branch committee. Of the nine female stewards who were members of the branch committee, eight held some post or posts on it. For male stewards the corresponding figures were twenty-two on the branch committee and sixteen of these twenty-two holding posts on the branch committee.

One of the important divisions in trade union experience, which was noticeable in interviews, was between those shop stewards whose understanding and knowledge of the union had essentially stayed at the departmental level and those who were also aware of branch level debate and issues. For some shop stewards, who only held office for a short time, and maybe had taken office because of specific

98

departmental problems, the department, not the branch or any regional or national structures, had been their source of knowledge about NALGO matters. Other shop stewards in interview, however, were well able to comment on levels of NALGO organization in other departments and on current debates in the branch, as well as having some views of NALGO's national policies. They were well on their way to becoming what Batstone *et al.* refer to as the 'quasi-elite', that is, the level of lay union activists from whom full-time union officials are likely to be recruited (Batstone, Boraston and Frenkel, 1977). This issue of knowledge of the union beyond the immediate departmental level is important if women are to achieve proportionate representation at all levels of the union. To develop a union 'career' requires knowledge of the union structures and procedures for standing for election, as well as an understanding of wider union politics.

Gender and Attitudes to Being a Shop Steward

In the questionnaire survey informants were asked a number of attitudinal questions about the role of the shop steward, including definition of a good shop steward, and the good and bad things about being a shop steward. These replies were cross-tabulated by sex to examine whether there was any relationship between gender and attitudes towards being a shop steward.

The question about views of what makes a good shop steward produced some gender differences. Ten women (45.5 per cent) and ten men (23.8 per cent) ranked as first choice 'a good shop steward is someone who keeps their members well-informed'. This suggests that women valued the information-passing role more than men. This may be because women obtained less information than men via their jobs about what was happening in terms of council employment policy or maybe it was an aspect of the shop steward role that women felt particularly competent and happy with. The comments later in this section by the (female) branch organizer about women stewards often being good organizers and administrators would fit in with this. Moreover it is possible that more women than men in council employment had jobs which involved passing on routine information.

The statement 'a good shop steward is someone who provides a lead to members' was not a popular response for either sex. Aiding membership participation was ranked slightly more highly by women than men with 18.2 per cent of the women and 14.3 per cent of the men placing this first. Being a good departmental representative was ranked first proportionately by more men (28.6 per cent) than women (4.5 per cent) although an equal number of men and women ranked it second. On the other hand, being good at sorting out grievances of members was ranked first by 22.7 per cent of the women and 14.3 per cent of the men. Maybe women were focusing here more on individual issues facing members rather than collective departmental issues.

A write-in question, where informants were invited to identify other characteristics of a good shop steward, produced a three-way split among the thirty-five informants who answered it. Twelve (four women and eight men) emphasized moral and personal qualities, eight (one woman and seven men) mentioned political awareness, and fifteen (eight women and seven men) referred to competence and effectiveness in performing union work. These responses suggest that the women who answered the question tended to reject the more politicized view of the shop steward role in favour of the competent representative role. This may reflect the fact that many women worked in jobs which did not offer the opportunity to perform any leadership roles.

Informants were also asked about the good and bad things about being a shop steward and these replies were cross-tabulated by sex. There appeared to be no gender difference in getting more information about NALGO, but this was not rated highly by either sex. Finding trade union work interesting was rated slightly more highly by women than men, with 27.3 per cent of the women and 9.5 per cent of the men ranking this first. It was ranked second by 22.7 per cent of the women and 28.6 per cent of the men. This corresponds with responses to the question about reasons for becoming a shop steward in the first place. These female shop stewards do not fit the traditional stereotype of women workers as uninterested in trade unionism.

The statement 'it makes me feel more confident' was not supported strongly by either sex, which is not surprising given the difficult climate for trade unions in the 1980s. Proportionately more women than men, however, did rank it highly, with 4.5 per cent of the women and 2.4 per cent of the men putting it first and 13.6 per cent of the women and 7.4 per cent of the men putting it second. Trade union activism was not, however, a significant empowering experience for either sex.

Sorting out members' problems was rated more highly by men than women as one of the positive aspects of being a shop steward. This was ranked first by 23.8 per cent of the men and 4.7 per cent of the women; 24.3 per cent of the men and 9.5 per cent of the women ranked it second. Maybe men's higher occupational status made it easier for them to do this successfully. Being successful in negotiations was rated first by 9.1 per cent of the women and 7.1 per cent of the men, with 27.3 per cent of the women and 14.3 per cent of the men ranking it second, so this aspect of being a shop steward was valued slightly more by women than men.

The statement 'I have learned a lot from being a shop steward' was ranked first by seven women (31.8 per cent) and eleven men (26.2 per cent), indicating that it was valued by a substantial proportion of each sex, but rather more so by women than men. This could reflect occupational status, in that higher-status males already had other sources of information, or gender role, in that women admit more readily than men to having learned things.

Questions about the bad things about being a shop steward also produced some gender differences. The statement 'it creates difficulties in doing one's job' was ranked more highly by men than women. This may reflect the fact that men had more senior jobs with more open-ended responsibilities. Because these jobs were more senior they were often more flexible, enabling the shop steward to do more union work in work time. Questions about the operation of union facility time suggest that trade union work created less difficulties for women than men in doing their job, because women did more union work in their own time.

The other statement which produced an interesting degree of gender difference was in response to the statement 'the responsibility can be worrying'. This was rated more highly by women than men: 22.7 per cent of the women and 9.5 per cent of the men put this first and 27.3 per cent of the women and 4.8 per cent of the men put it second. This may reflect the fact that women worry more than men or that they find it easier than men to admit to worrying. This point is discussed in the interview extract from the (female) branch organizer below. If women do worry more than men, this may reflect greater conscientiousness, but this can be a factor which holds women back in union activity, if it makes them reluctant to take on more senior union responsibilities.

In the interviews with branch officers and shop stewards some qualitative material on gender roles in relation to union office-holding was obtained. Some of this will be discussed later in this chapter and in Chapter 6. Material reproduced here deals with gender differences in performance of the shop steward role.

One female branch organizer discussed the problems for women of performing the shop steward role in the following terms:

It's I think partly the nature of women to be more self-critical. I can only say that I am, whereas some of my colleagues who are men will not agonize so much over whether they are doing something well, they just do the best they can, and I don't mean that they don't think about it, whereas I will spend hours agonizing over something. Maybe men do still agonize in the same way, but probably for reasons to do with upbringing and everything else, they don't show it in that way. Whereas women, as a result of their being brought up not to be decision-makers, I mean that's the critical bit, not to be people of action, I don't think women have traditionally been people of action, they've been brought up into a more passive role. Therefore when they're put into an action situation, in a decision-making situation, it is for women more difficult, not impossible, just more difficult.

This self-critical quality, while it could help women to do union work better than men, could also act as a barrier to taking union office in the first place, or encourage female shop stewards to step down. What is interesting, however, about the analysis of gender roles is that it is not easy to decide whether men are equally uncertain about particular decisions, since the gender role difference may lie in concealing anxiety rather than not experiencing it. She also felt that women's socialization could affect performance in particular aspects of the shop steward role, namely meetings, although in administration and organization she had generally found women to be at least as competent as men.

I think that the issues that women find more difficult to deal with are not dealing with individuals, but dealing with meetings. Pressure gets put on you at meetings, whether union meetings or negotiating meetings. Because in their jobs women haven't necessarily had experience of that, and the union work puts you into the position where you meet across the table with your chief officer, but you meet as an equal when you're a shop steward, and that is a role I think women find more difficult to move into than men.

This statement indicates well the interrelation of gender role and occupational status in affecting women's union work.

Table 5.7: Experience of Industrial Action as a Member of NALGO — Male and Female Shop Stewards

Form of Industrial Action	Male Shop Stewards	Female Shop Stewards
Overtime ban	23.8%	36.4%
Work-to-rule	19.0%	31.8%
No cover of vacant posts	61.9%	45.5%
Ban on use of telephones	21.4%	13.6%
Refusal to take on new duties	33.3%	40.1%
Ban on talking to councillors	28.6%	4.5%
Ban on use of cars for work purposes	14.3%	13.6%
Half-day strike	54.8%	40.9%
One-day strike	66.7%	50.0%
Strike lasting under one week	9.5%	0.0%
Strike lasting one week to one month	2.4%	0.0%
Strike lasting one to three months	9.5%	13.6%
Strike lasting over three months	4.8%	4.5%

Gender and Industrial Action

In the questionnaire survey, informants were asked about their experiences of industrial action. At the time of the survey, which was before the national NALGO strikes of 1989, eighteen female stewards (81.8 per cent) and thirty-five male stewards (83.3 per cent) had taken part in some form of industrial action. Table 5.7 gives the percentages of male and female shop stewards taking part in a variety of forms of industrial action.

The largest gender differences here related either to strike action or the ban on talking to councillors. Much of the variation in levels of strike action can be explained in terms of departmental factors, since much strike action occurred at departmental rather than branch level. Involvement in the ban on talking to councillors was related to job status, since higher-status jobs were more likely to involve servicing council committees and dealing with queries from councillors (see Chapter 4). Thus these figures do not indicate any particular gender role difference in willingness to take industrial action.

In the interviews some comments were made on women's experiences of industrial action. These did not indicate any lack of preparedness on the part of women to take part in industrial action. They did, however, indicate ways in which women's gender role could be used against them when taking industrial action. For instance during the nursery nurses' regrading campaign one of the leading shop stewards in the campaign explained how industrial action by women in a caring job was often perceived critically.

> At nearly every meeting we went to out of Sheffield we were always put under pressure by people who turned round and said to us, more or less, 'You are women and you are taking industrial action against children and families'. They played on it several times to say we were women and we shouldn't be taking industrial action against parents and children and made us feel bad.

What is being raised here is a conflict between a traditional feminine gender role, caring for children, and the rights of workers to take industrial action. The statement shows the inner conflicts this produced for the union activists. On the one hand they felt they were being unfairly guilt-tripped, but on another level they still felt hurt by these criticisms. The need to withstand these pressures against taking industrial action is a factor which affects some women workers and some workers in particular 'caring' occupations. It is entirely possible, for instance, that a male residential social worker might feel similar conflicts about taking industrial action. I did not, however, encounter any male interviewees who talked about feeling guilty whether about taking time off for union work, taking industrial action or any other aspect of their working or personal lives.

Another shop steward, who had been involved in the new technology dispute, referred to the lack of sympathy for lower-grade female staff when taking industrial action, from male union colleagues, many of whom were in managerial positions.

> There were staff in the Treasury who didn't believe we should be out on strike. . . . In the Treasury men tend to be in higher-profile jobs, higher-graded jobs, and the women tend to be in the lower-graded jobs. The new technology comes into the job more when you are on the lower-graded job, so the managers, who are mostly males, couldn't understand what all the fuss was about. (Female ex-shop steward)

This statement illustrates how both gender and occupational inequalities tended to undermine union solidarity when low-graded women workers were taking industrial action over issues of specific concern to them. On the other hand, the national NALGO strike of 1989 in defence of national pay rates and national bargaining had been a unifying dispute, in which women had played an active role. This experience had been empowering for many women involved. As one of the female shop stewards stated:

> On the picket lines [in the 1989 national strike] the best picket organizers were women in this department. (Female shop steward in Housing)

Gender and Union Facility Agreements

The practical difficulties of the operation of the trade union facilities agreement have already been indicated in Chapter 4, namely that while stewards were entitled to leave their jobs to do union work, there was usually no cover for the work they left. For some jobs cover was essential to allow stewards to leave the job to do union work. One of the nursery nurse shop stewards described the particular problems of her job as follows:

> *Is it difficult being a shop steward doing a job like a nursery nurse?*
> Yes, it's extremely difficult, because you can't actually have time off work without cover, that's where the cost is. We did come to an agreement with the Education Department for cover. It is difficult because you are not dealing with paper-work, you're dealing with young children. Nursery nurses work in a team situation with a teacher and another nursery nurse and I couldn't leave them without cover because (a) the children weren't in a safe environment and (b) it puts extra pressure on the staff you leave, which you really don't want to do. What you need is continuity for the children as well. It's no good having different people in to cover every day or every week, because children need to see the same face and you have a routine in the nursery and it takes time for someone to get into that routine and to know the children. If you don't get someone who is familiar to them it puts extra work on the nursery staff who remain. (Nursery nurse shop steward)

This shop steward was able to sort out her cover problems because she had a regular person, who wanted part-time work, who was employed to cover for her. She stressed that she also worked with an understanding head-teacher and staff. A number of women interviewees

Table 5.8: *Hours per Week Spent on NALGO Work, by Gender*

Number of Hours	Male Shop Stewards	Female Shop Stewards
0–5 hours	33.3%	27.3%
6–10 hours	33.3%	45.5%
11–15 hours	11.9%	9.1%
16–20 hours	11.9%	9.1%
Over 20 hours	4.8%	9.1%

Table 5.9: *Times when Union Work Performed, by Gender*

Times when Union Work Performed	Male Shop Stewards	Female Shop Stewards
Mostly in work time	59.5%	31.8%
About half in work time and half in own time	35.7%	54.5%
Mostly in own time	4.8%	13.6%

emphasized the importance of supportive work colleagues. This account indicates the need in some jobs not only for cover to do union work, but for a type of cover which is appropriate to the job and allows the post-holder to leave the job without being concerned that the work is not being done properly in her absence. In a way the situation of the nursery nurse shop steward needing good quality cover for her work is similar to working parents needing good quality childcare, so that they can go to work without worrying about the children.

In the interview schedule, informants were asked a number of questions about the operation of union facility agreements and the relation between job and union work.

Table 5.8 does not indicate any major gender difference in the amount of time spent on union work. There were, however, substantial gender differences in the time when this union work was done, as table 5.9 shows. This shows that union facility agreements were working less well for female shop stewards than for male shop stewards. This is partly a matter of job status.

In the questionnaire survey, informants were asked whether they had any problems taking time off for union work and whether their job assisted their union work and whether it conflicted in any way with it. By looking at the answers to these questions, broken down by

Table 5.10: *Difficulties in Taking Time Off for Union Work, by Gender*

Do you encounter any difficulties in taking the time off work for union duties which you are formally allowed to take?

	Male Shop Stewards	**Female Shop Stewards**
YES	28.6%	40.9%
NO	66.7%	59.1%
DON'T KNOW	4.8%	0.0%

Table 5.11: *Sources of Difficulty in Taking Time Off for Union Work, by Gender*

	Value of Ranking		
	First Ranking	Second Ranking	Third Ranking
Male Shop Stewards:			
Source of Difficulty			
Pressure from managers	9.5%	4.8%	2.4%
Pressure from colleagues	2.4%	9.5%	2.4%
Pressure from service users	9.5%	0.0%	2.4%
Other factors (usually workload)	19.0%	2.4%	4.8%
Female Shop Stewards:			
Source of Difficulty			
Pressure from managers	22.7%	0.0%	0.0%
Pressure from colleagues	0.0%	9.1%	13.6%
Pressure from service users	4.5%	13.6%	4.5%
Other factors (usually workload)	22.7%	4.5%	0.0%

gender, we can explore more fully the reasons why women did more of their union work in their own time than men did.

Slightly more women than men reported that they did have difficulties in taking time off for union work, as table 5.10 shows.

Even though many informants stated that they had no difficulty taking time off for union work, some did give later questionnaire responses which indicated some sources of difficulty. There is a noticeable gender difference (table 5.11) in response to 'pressure from managers'. For female stewards this came first as often as other factors, such as workload pressure. It was clearly more of a problem for female than male stewards, reflecting job status and perhaps attitudes of managers to union activity on the part of women workers.

Table 5.12 shows minimal gender difference in access to information and acquisition of skills which are useful for union work. The other three categories, access to members, job flexibility and access to

Table 5.12: *Job Support for Union Work, by Gender*

Form of Support	Male Shop Stewards	Female Shop Stewards
Giving access to useful information	61.9%	59.1%
Allowing easy access to members	88.1%	59.1%
Giving flexibility in organizing time and work	85.7%	68.2%
Helping develop skills useful in union work (e.g. public speaking, organizing meetings)	52.4%	50.0%
Giving access to senior management	64.3%	40.9%

Table 5.13: *Job Conflicts with Union Work, by Gender*

Form of Conflict	Male Shop Stewards	Female Shop Stewards
Conflict of time demands	83.3%	68.2%
Threat to promotion prospects	59.5%	50.0%
Problem of building up a backlog of work	61.9%	63.6%
Inflexibility of work	9.5%	13.6%
Conflict of responsibilities/loyalties (wearing two hats)	45.2%	45.5%

senior management, show greater differences between men's and women's work situation. In all three cases men's jobs were providing greater assistance to the performance of union work than women's.

The one noticeable gender difference in table 5.13 was that men felt conflict of time demands more than women (83.3 per cent compared with 68.2 per cent), although it was strongly identified as a problem by both sexes. The fact that men experienced this to a greater degree than women may be related to the fact that men made greater use of union facility agreements and did less union work in their own time.

Interviews provided further material about the problems of taking time off for union work. This allowed some exploration of gender differences in attitudes towards work and union facility time. Some shop stewards clearly found it easier to be assertive about their rights to time off for union work. This relates to occupational status, departmental culture and gender role. Where a gender difference could be discerned it appeared that in some ways women were more work-oriented than men, in that they were less willing to let job performance be affected by union work.

One male branch officer described how as a shop steward he had been able to adjust his workload to fit in the union work:

> When I first started as a shop steward, one of the things that a careers officer was supposed to do was to read various bits of literature and so on about new jobs etc., so that was the first thing that went, but obviously that isn't noticeable, whereas if I was on the reception desk, then it's a lot more difficult to say 'Well I'm going off for two hours and leaving nobody on the reception desk'. (Male branch officer)

Many male interviewees, who were aware that job status and job flexibility enabled them to fit union work into work time, recognized and identified the contrast between their situation and that of other workers. A male chief shop steward described his work situation as a computer adviser as follows:

> I have got such a flexible job that I don't have any trouble at all. If something's rescheduled then something gets put back another week and we lose a week. The work piles up on my desk, but it just gets rescheduled. Timescales of projects can be shoved back as a result of the work that I do for the union. It's a bit more difficult for a departmental secretary or a clerk-typist in the typing pool, where everybody gets a big pile of work and she's still got a bit left, then they're going to increase the amount they throw on top of that. She's bound to be under pressure to keep the same sort of productivity as everyone else. There was a steward at one time who actually worked hard until quarter past five to make up the time when she was off as a shop steward so that her work didn't fall behind, which I suppose someone feels they have to do, but I'm not very happy about it.

As these extracts indicate, for workers (who were mostly women) in clerical, secretarial and reception jobs obtaining time off for union work was very difficult unless cover was available. Many interviewees commented on the necessity of cover and attempts by the branch to negotiate it, but they recognized the difficulty of achieving this. In some professional jobs, too, it was difficult or impossible at times to use the union facility agreement. This is illustrated in the following account from a female ex-shop steward in F&CS.

There was no problem about getting time off to go to meetings. No one said 'You can't go', but getting the job covered
was difficult. I was working in a small unit which had to be
covered at all times, working with mentally handicapped people.
So sometimes I just couldn't leave the job. It wouldn't be fair
on the other workers or the people we were looking after in
the unit. Sometimes it's just not possible to leave.
*So did you feel a conflict between doing your job and union
work?*
Yes at times I did. It's important to represent people and
generally people appreciate what you're doing, but you're still
missing from the unit. I decided not to stand again as a shop
steward partly because I had sorted out the problem which
was the initial reason for standing, and partly because I wanted
to concentrate my energies on work more. I felt unhappy that
I was not doing my job as well as I could because of the amount
of time necessary for the union work. And when you're looking after vulnerable clients who need support you want to put
your time into doing the job properly.

The following interview indicates also the differences in the
position of different grades of women workers in respect of operating
the union facilities agreement.

Whereas in my own case because I was in a managerial position I was able to sort out my own workload and when I did
my work, so I was able to do trade union duties and when I
became chief shop steward I was then seconded for three days.
I had three days that I could use for trade union duties and
somebody was put in to cover my job. (Female branch officer)

Gender and Shop Steward Turnover

The relation of trade union facility agreements to shop steward turnover has been discussed earlier, in Chapter 4. It is reasonable to suppose that shop stewards who can do a substantial amount of union
work in work time are more likely to stand again for election, and to
stay in office over a number of years, than those who feel obliged to
do much union work in their own time.
    An analysis of the annual list of shop stewards showed that,
averaged across departments, there was no gender difference in the

rate of shop steward turnover. The average length of service as a shop steward for both sexes was two years. The figures showed that the great majority of shop stewards only serve for one or two years, while only a minority serve for several years and so are more likely to accumulate the union expertise which enables them to take on branch office and regional and national union positions.

In interviews, I endeavoured to find out whether informants thought male and female shop stewards stood down for different reasons. A great variety of reasons were offered for shop steward turnover; these included workloads, promotion or job change, ability to find a replacement as shop steward, activism related to a single issue which subsided when that issue was resolved, childcare responsibilities, and the pressures of union work. There was no conclusive evidence that men and women resigned for different reasons, although it is possible that more female stewards stood down because of pressures of work and difficulties of getting time off, while more men were promoted out of union work.

Management Harassment of Female Union Officers and Stewards

In two of the in-depth interviews with female union activists, one of whom was a branch officer and ex-chief shop steward and the other of whom was ex-branch president, the issue of management harassment of female union activists was raised by the interviewee. What was described was a form of sexist harassment, in which women union activists encountered employment discrimination and a hostile reception from the managers they had to negotiate with. Both informants referred to an organizational culture in which trade union activity was seen as 'unfeminine' and not suitable for women. One spoke of 'institutionalized sexism'. They both noted that behaviour which was seen as assertiveness on the part of men was viewed as aggression when engaged in by women. Thus they felt men tended to get promoted as a result of trade union activism, while women were denied promotion as a result of it, and that this discouraged other women from taking on union office.

These were both informants with substantial experience in the branch. What they identify is a serious problem for trade unions seeking to increase participation of women members. It is not always easy for unions to protect activists against discrimination by management.

Where this discrimination takes the form of sex discrimination as well, it is also potentially divisive of the membership.

> I think women are discriminated against when they are shop stewards, because it is not seen as a feminine activity, if you are assertive you are seen as being aggressive whereas for men that's seen as being forceful and not aggressive, and men shop stewards, I'm speaking from experience here, men tend to be promoted whereas women don't. I was chief shop steward for three years, a job I thoroughly enjoyed doing, but I also feel that I have been discriminated against because I was chief shop steward and that it's held me back.
>   I think that women are viewed, in fact I know that some women are viewed, who are assertive when they are trade union officers, as aggressive. I don't see myself that way and I don't think my members see me that way, but unfortunately when you are negotiating with men and you say 'This is the corporate policy, this is what will be followed', then that's how you're viewed.
> *So does this discourage other women?*
> Yes I think so, yes, they don't see other women being promoted, they have to pick something up from that. (Female branch officer and ex-chief shop steward)

The other interviewee linked the issue of management discrimination against female union activists to the council's equal opportunities code and also identified a very different treatment of male and female union activists.

> The women who were shop stewards actually got stamped on almost openly. I'm aware of many women who feel they've been denied promotion because of their trade union activity, whereas men have got promotion almost because of their trade union activity. I know of three women who have taken out grievances that they have been discriminated against because of their union activity. I know of one man and he got promoted, the three women didn't. There is an issue there with the council about how it implements its commitment not to discriminate against people on the grounds of trade union activity [part of the council's equal opportunities code of practice]. They actually treat men and women differently in the way that they discriminate or the way they view trade

union activity. Men are more likely to be promoted, women are more likely to be pushed down. (Female shop steward, ex-branch president)

She also indicated that even if the union members were free of gender stereotypes, these were still held by the managers whom union representatives had to negotiate with and this constituted a problem for female union office-holders.

If you're a woman you're not assertive, you're aggressive. I think it is an issue about it not being a feminine thing to do.

Union Activism and Maintaining a Personal Life

Stress at work is increasingly recognized as a social problem. For union activists the stresses of work can be compounded by the stresses of union work. Stresses related to union activity have been addressed in some trade union courses (Labour Research Department, 1988a). Some of these courses have included personal coping strategies, such as co-counselling and assertiveness training. The Labour Research Department quotes the NUPE Northern Divisional Education Officer as saying the courses on stress for trade unionists 'manage to link personal issues and personal problems with collective bargaining and other negotiating issues' (p. 17).

This linkage of the personal and the collective issues is important for unions in helping to sustain long-term activism. As already indicated in the section on shop steward turnover, many shop stewards stayed in office for only one or two years. While this was often related to work pressures, other aspects of personal life may also have been relevant. One obvious aspect is childcare responsibilities. The questionnaire stage of the research indicated the virtual absence of women with young children as union office-holders. Some men tended to reduce their levels of union activity when they became fathers. One male branch officer stopped being an officer for a year after the birth of twins. Another male shop steward decided to resign as a steward when he and his wife arranged to job-share following the birth of their second child.

The operation of the union facilities agreement also needs to be considered. The more shop stewards were obliged to use their own time for union duties, the less free time they had for social and personal life. One male shop steward, who had been a shop steward for six years at the time of the survey, described how because of changes in his job he was now able to do more union work in work time.

> I noticed one of the questions on the form was about the amount of work you do at home compared to the amount of work you do in your own time and for me that's changed. When I started being a steward I used to do a lot of work at home, because I could do writing letters, word-processing, writing documents etc., more easily at home because of access to a printer. But as the years have gone by I've found more opportunity to do that sort of thing at work. I do [union] work on databases and word-processing at work and so I tend to spend hardly any time on union work outside work hours, apart from the union meetings in the evenings.
> *Has that made it easier to continue as a shop steward?*
> I think so. (Male shop steward)

Much material emerged in interviews from both male and female shop stewards, and even more so from the branch officers, about the personal costs and stresses of union activism. Interviewees stressed the necessity of being single or having very supportive partners and having no children or grown-up children. Also, the branch officers were a tight-knit group who provided moral support for each other's union activism. The following interview extracts illustrate this:

> A lot of people in senior positions in the branch, although not all, are often people who are divorced, separated or have got very understanding partners or who can't stand the sight of their partners, rather than people who have so-called normal relationships. In my opinion that runs through the hierarchy of lay officials at district and national level, so it's much more difficult for a so-called normal married relationship to be able to function. (Male branch officer)

> How does it [union activism] affect my personal life? Well I think it's bad news basically . . . because if something needs doing for the union then personal lives inevitably end up taking the brunt of that. You end up not doing personal-life-type things; you have to do union things at the weekend and in the evenings, and that is not a good thing. (Male chief shop steward)

> Unfortunately most of the activists in the branch tend to be divorced, separated. I don't know if this is where trade unionism

leads you. But that's how it appears to be. It really does almost take over your life, because it doesn't just involve the work here in the branch, I mean you have to go to meetings, there's meetings at district, in London, which I went to on Friday, there's district council which meets on a Saturday, there's Annual Conference which is a week away and so on. (Female branch officer)

Informants remarked that it was not only the time demands of union work that they found stressful and restrictive of personal life, but also the tendency to take union work home with them mentally. This occurred particularly if they were dealing with difficult casework, such as final stage disciplinaries, or were handling major issues in negotiations. Indeed, one shop steward commented that it was just like jobs such as teaching and social work in that it was not possible to switch off mentally from the job, that is the union work, when one went home.

You tend to take it home with you a lot of the time, while it may not be work that you take home, it's all in your head and it's going round your head while you're at home. (Female branch officer)

Another informant observed that the problems of the stresses of union work increased the longer someone held union office:

The longer you're active in the union, the more experienced people expect you to be. It's an ever-growing circle. The longer you do it, the more demand there's going to be for you to do more. (Female shop steward)

In comments about ways of coping with the stress of union work informants talked about both the need at times for solitude and also the importance of socializing with other activists.

I do need a lot of time on my own, to recover from the stresses, otherwise you just start suffering from burn-out and you don't want to pick anything up and you start getting sloppy. (Female branch officer)

The present group of branch officers have been branch officers together for the last year and so it is a close group, so we tend

> to socialize as well together so it's very much union, union, union. I personally think I couldn't do this job without that sort of support from the other branch officers. (Female branch officer)

> Socially the people I mix with are people who would support trade union activity. (Female shop steward)

While much of the interview material indicated the stresses of union work, and interviewees did at times refer to union work as a 'thankless task', this should not be taken to imply that activists gained no personal and psychological benefits from activism. Some activists did hold union office for a number of years. This cannot be explained only in terms of inability to find a replacement as shop steward or pressure from colleagues to continue in office. The main reasons for continuing in office on a long-term basis seemed to be either that people enjoyed union work on balance or that they had some political consciousness which made union work relevant and important to them. As one long-standing shop steward put it:

> Because I am a political activist then my trade union will always be the natural starting point for my political activism. (Male shop steward)

Women at Branch Officer Level

One of the issues about the stresses of union work which was discussed in interviews was whether they were different for men and women or not. On the one hand, shop stewards and union officers of both sexes recognized that the responsibility of union work could be worrying, particularly when dealing with casework where members' jobs were at stake. Pressures on personal time were also identified as a problem for both sexes. On the other hand, there was a recognition that if women were in traditional relationships with men there might be less tolerance of their union activism by their partners than their male colleagues might receive from their partners. As one male branch officer acknowledged:

> Pressures of union work can affect men and women equally. If a woman decides to become active she can be placed under the same pressures that the man who decides to become active

is. But as a generalization I think it's probably true to say that there are more men who are active at senior levels than women. A woman might find it more difficult than a man to take on the role of union officer. In certain relationships there's still that kind of traditional role that a woman should do more round the house and so on which allows the male to get away with spending more time in the union at higher level, whereas a woman who becomes involved at higher level, if she's married or living with a more traditional partner, might find herself under more pressure than the average man. So in certain situations it affects people equally, in other situations it can affect women disproportionately.

In fact none of the female branch officers interviewed appeared to be in a 'traditional' relationship. Indeed one of the female branch officers, when speaking about the importance of personal space and the need for solitude at times, recognized that her situation was in some ways different from that of many people in allowing her to be alone. She stated:

> I'm fortunate that I can go home and be on my own, when lots
> of people can't. (Female branch officer)

This is not the conventional social view of women living alone, but may be one which is appropriate to many women who hold responsible positions in work and other organizations.

There was also a degree of support for each other among the women branch officers, although being supportive was not confined to one sex, as one female branch officer stated.

> There are three women officers in the branch now. We do act
> as support for each other, but having said that there are male
> branch officers who are equally supportive.

Among the male branch officers who were identified as supportive of women branch officers was the male international relations officer, who was the one black officer in the branch.

In one case one of the female shop stewards, who had been a branch officer, was living with one of the male branch officers. This presented her, although not, it appeared, him, with the problem of maintaining a separate identity within the branch. She had to work hard to establish respect for herself as an activist in her own right.

I don't know whether you know that the executive officer and I live together. When I stood as branch president I actually made a statement that I'd been in NALGO longer than he has. If I'm going to make mistakes at least give me credit for making my own mistakes and not for making his mistakes for him. Give me the credit for having a brain of my own. I can actually work out where I stand on things without just assuming that I'm parroting off what he thinks. I think people see him as the person who influences me and not the other way round. Nobody thinks that I influence him. I think I do and he thinks I do.

In Chapter 2, the existing research on women union leaders at local and national level was discussed. As already mentioned, most women who had reached this level of union office did not have childcare responsibilities and many of them were single. These personal characteristics tended to be similar for the women officers interviewed in my research. In total, six senior women activists were interviewed. These were the branch organizer (a NALGO employee), and five branch officers or ex-officers. The posts these women held at the time of the research or previously were:

shop steward, branch organizer
shop steward, chief shop steward and welfare officer
shop steward and publicity officer
shop steward, education officer and service conditions officer
shop steward service conditions officer, equal opportunities officer
shop steward, equal opportunities officer, branch president.

At the time of the questionnaire study of the shop steward population there were three female branch officers (welfare, publicity and shop stewards organizer).

One issue explored in interviews was whether women tended to take on certain roles within the branch committee doing administrative and support jobs rather than taking offices which involved negotiating and up-front leadership positions. There were ten branch officer positions in total. These were branch secretary, executive officer, two service conditions officers, shop stewards organizer, equal opportunities officer, publicity officer, welfare officer, education officer, and international relations officer. The female union officer who moved from being service conditions officer to equal opportunities officer remarked that she felt she had more authority within the branch as a service conditions officer. The female officer who moved from being education officer to service conditions officer did so because she recognized the importance of women being involved in collective bargaining to advance union policies on women's rights.

The welfare officer felt that her job was not stereotyped within the branch as a woman's job, although it was the type of job that could easily have been viewed in that way.

So how much does the gender matter when it comes to the branch officers? whence.

Not at all. I think we've got over that hurdle. They tend to slip into it sometimes. 'This is a woman's job', they're very soon pulled back.

Right, now at the moment you're a branch officer with responsibility for welfare. Can you tell me a bit about that work?

Well, the welfare officer deals with people who need to go on convalescent and that covers retired members as well, people who have financial problems — the union office helps people like that. And anybody who needs any form of counselling, but it's a job that you have to do on your own, because it's a very confidential job. So any of the work that I carry out isn't discussed with any other branch officers, which is a departure because we have branch officers' meetings and discuss what every other branch officer is doing but mine remains confidential.

Is it seen as a woman's job perhaps?

I don't think so, not in this branch. I mean the previous welfare officer to me was a man so I would hate to categorize it into gender roles, but I do think it does happen that we don't have a woman service conditions officer, which we probably should have. We don't have and never have had a woman executive officer, we will in the future I'm sure.

Are you going to stand for some of these jobs?

I will I'm sure.

But some of those jobs are seen as more masculine jobs, are they?

Oh yes.

Is that still part of the macho thing about negotiating?

Yes it is, but it is also again the knock-on effect of most women in the authority being in lower-paid jobs and the business of sitting down and negotiating with directors or the chief executive

> or the chief personnel officer, if you're not used to dealing
> with those sorts of individuals in your job, then it can be a bit
> daunting to go in and to start negotiating with them. (Female
> branch officer)

What this interview reveals is again the interrelation of gender role
and occupational status in affecting women's union participation. Once
women had got over the initial hurdles, however, they had the confidence to contemplate going on to hold other union posts.

Several of the senior female officers were conscious of their situation as possible role models for other women in the branch. Role
models were seen as important in encouraging other women to become union activists:

> We're lacking a few role models at the moment. There are not
> many women branch officers who are prominent.
> *Were you a role model when you were branch president?*
> I think to some extent yes, I think I was when I was a shop
> steward too. There were women activists in F&CS who were
> very much in the forefront of what was happening, and I think
> that it is important. I think role models are. (Female shop
> steward, ex-branch president)

Another female branch officer commented on the importance to her
of role models in her development into the union activist she had
become.

> *Did you have any role models that helped you?*
> Yes, my mother — very much so. She wasn't active within the
> unions, but she was a very assertive woman and was very
> political, still does have strong political views so it was always
> okay for me. It always felt okay to be involved in political
> activities. I was always encouraged to think that as a woman I
> could do anything and I think that has great bearing.

In some cases the role model position was actively accepted by the
officer concerned, while in others it was recognized rather more
hesitantly.

> The way I see myself is trying to act as a role model to encour-
> age more women to become active in the political sphere.
> (Female branch officer)

Do you think women in your position act as a role model for other women too?
I wouldn't like to say yes, but I think probably they do. It's been said to me by women 'Well I saw you do that' or 'I saw you talk at that meeting and I thought well if she can do it I can' and that does rub off, but I don't set myself up as a role model. (Female branch organizer)

Being a role model does, however, place an additional responsibility on a woman union officer.

And does being a role model put particular pressure on women officers to do things extra well?
Yes, yes I constantly feel as if I'm on show, and that if I make a mistake then it's a glaring mistake, and it isn't but it's just that internally that's how you feel.

Given this additional pressure on women officers it is useful to consider why women continued as union officers. Some mentioned the importance of supportive union friends. Others had also changed jobs, partly as a result of union work, and had moved into jobs which made union activism easier, a survival strategy also adopted by some male activists. One ex-nursery nurse shop steward had moved upwards into an administrative job which was more flexible than her previous work. Moreover, once shop stewards reached branch officer level they received cover for their union work. Another reason for continuing given by one of the female officers interviewed was involvement in new issues combined with a commitment to using the trade union to advance equal rights.

I mean in my own case it's becoming more of an involvement in corporate issues and in issues that affect women, trying to push those issues to the front of the agenda. I mean I'm heavily involved at the moment in working with the authority and trying to draw up a new procedure for sexual and racial harassment, how we can take those cases forward. So it's a lot of the time if it's something very dear to you, a cause that you espouse and you can get involved in it then you tend to stay a steward much longer. (Female branch officer)

NALGO's Attempts to Promote Women's Participation and Representation in the Union

Besides the role model function assumed by some of the women branch officers, the NALGO branch had taken a number of measures to increase women's participation in the branch. These included the provision of childcare facilities for union meetings and attempts to negotiate cover for shop stewards. In addition the branch had developed its equal opportunities work, which will be discussed in Chapter 6.

Several interviewees mentioned the childcare provision made by the branch. This consisted not only of creches at meetings but also the payment of childcare expenses where this was a more appropriate form of provision. In comparative terms this placed the branch among the more progressive of union organizations on this issue. While the case for creches at union meetings has been won in many sectors of the trade union movement, following feminist campaigning in the 1970s and 1980s, payment of childcare expenses is still less widespread. The practical operation of this policy is illustrated in the following extracts from interviews:

> Childcare expenses can be claimed for union work. A creche is provided at branch meetings and is used. The branch secretary is responsible for organizing the creche — and forgot once. (Female branch officer)

> The branch does try to help shop stewards with young children by first of all providing creches at the special general meetings and annual general meetings. Some years ago it was agreed that shop stewards could actually claim for a person to look after the kids at home if for example they had a meeting to go to in the evening. I'm not sure whether everybody knows about it. I claim it sometimes because I've got twins and ironically as a male I benefit from it, where I think it was originally intended to help women. It was actually the women in the branch who pushed for it. (Male branch officer)

The type of childcare provision made by the branch indicated an understanding that taking children to creches is not always convenient or suitable for the needs of children. One male shop steward commented on the problem as follows:

> We ought to do something about the problem of members with young children, but it is easier said than done. We can

provide childcare for the period of the branch executive once a month, but if I had children I would be reluctant to have a kid of mine in a creche from half past four until seven o'clock. It would be particularly tiring for a 5-year-old. It wouldn't do the children any good. I'm sure there's quite a lot of people who feel like that. (Male chief shop steward)

Another problem particularly for parents related to the timing of meetings. Most branch meetings were held at 5.30 p.m. directly after work. This was the time which obtained the best attendance from members, but was difficult for parents. The problem of selecting a time for union meetings was illustrated in the following statement from one of the branch organizers interviewed.

There has been a debate in NALGO about the timing of branch meetings. They are usually at 5.30 p.m. with a creche provided. Some meetings, e.g. for nursery nurses and education clerks are held at 7.30 p.m. Their members are good attenders at 7.30 p.m. 5.30 p.m. is a good time for someone who works in the Town Hall, who would not come back for 7.30 p.m. Departmental meetings and some branch committees take place at lunch time. (Male branch organizer)

In some departments attempts were made to negotiate cover for shop stewards who were in jobs which it was difficult to leave to do union work. Given the inflexibility of some women's jobs, such a move would increase women's opportunities to be active in NALGO, and it was to a considerable extent understood in those terms.

In F&CS we have lately been negotiating with the director to set up a system to cover people involved in union work in some instances, where it's clear that the only way that time can be allowed is through cover being provided. That is currently happening with respect to one steward. (Male chief shop steward)

Lastly some women in the branch had thought about the traditional ways of running union meetings and whether they were appropriate as ways of organizing women workers. The female branch organizer recounted her experience of a meeting of the nursery nurses and childcare assistants.

It was a meeting in the council chamber of approximately 150 women. It was a meeting run by women with a completely different atmosphere to any other union meeting I've ever been in. The meeting wasn't run on traditional dictatorial lines where members when they were asking things were told 'No you can't discuss that now because that's item five on the agenda'. The shop stewards who were running the meeting allowed the members more leeway, so they had more freedom of expression. People were able to say what they thought, even if wasn't really quite the item they were speaking on. What I found was that by the end of that first meeting and subsequent meetings I attended all the issues that were on the agenda for discussion did get discussed and debated, but not necessarily in the order that was set down on the paper. Now the bureaucracy of unions tends to mirror the bureaucracy of the service that we work in. So unions are very structured in terms of how they discuss issues. When you take the case of the nursery nurses, who are virtually 100 per cent women, who have not got that history of meetings because it's not part of their work or part of their life, they approach it in a totally different way. The union organization needs to actually reflect the needs of the members and not impose on them 'this is the structure and this is the committee and the agenda and you will stick to the agenda'. (Female branch organizer)

What is noticeable about this account is that the branch organizer was able to learn from the members and was willing to let members experiment with different ways of organizing. She did not take the attitude that the members, who were new to union activism, were incompetent and needed training in the proper procedures, as the more traditional type of male union organizer might have done. Her account is an example of what Feldberg (1987) refers to as the need for unions to incorporate women's culture in their organizing strategies.

This account contrasts interestingly with the comments of one of the shop stewards on a national NALGO women's conference she attended. She found much of the NALGO structure at the conference rather bureaucratic and questioned whether it would involve women who were not already activists.

How do you see women's position in the union? Do NALGO's attempts to involve women have any impact?
In terms of the straightforward practical things like providing

344.0465 GRE

331.880942 BRI
331.880942 BRI

331.215 DEX

942.081 GRE

942.081 GRE

814.3 RUS.

301.424 COU.

331.4 WOM?

677.0285. ENG

305.5620793
WOR.

331.6 WORE.

Name:

Answer th[e]
with the as[

USING OF

1. Which
   a parti[c]

2. What is
   Kegley

992.081 GRE

8 28.3 .

301 . 912 GRE .

324 . 30942/STR

331 . 92 WOM ,

331 . 4 WOM .

nterscience: London.

ILL

ls, seeds of human futures.

3) <u>Conference on Design</u>

and the DIA. Design Council.

ILL

(all/new) Universal Traveler

-NIP. Crisp Publications

nguin.

V 4LL

cy. Design Council.

The Architectural Press,

L 1OWL; WV 1LL

gn Teaching Aids. Design

n. Design Council. (1984)

J 2 OWL; WV 3LL

on. Design Council.

LL

:Materials, Methods and

a creche, yes. Things like a women's committee don't particularly have an impact. I went to the NALGO women's conference. One of the things that was disappointing about it was that it was so bureaucratic. The starting level was we've got to have these district women's committees. Now no one's going to go along to that if they are not well and truly enmeshed in the shop steward system already. So you can't say that it pulls more women into activity, because it doesn't. I think there are things about the union structure that everyone finds off-putting, not just women. (Female shop steward)

Another interviewee, however, viewed the women's conference as a more successful event, recognizing the union-related barriers to women's participation that can exist.

Some women also find it very difficult to be in what is a male-dominated group, because trade unionism is very male-dominated.
NALGO's idea of a women's conference was that it was just women. So it made a very safe environment for women who aren't used to public speaking to get up and to say what they wanted to say. (Female branch officer)

What these interview accounts show is that branch officers and senior stewards were aware of some of the factors restricting women's participation in unions. There was recognition of the responsibilities of the union to provide what assistance could be given in terms of childcare provision, sensitive timing and conduct of meetings and negotiating for cover for union work.

Conclusion

The research findings shed some light on the processes of women's representation at various levels within the union. Under-representation at shop steward level was related to childcare responsibilities and to low occupational status, which made it difficult to exercise rights to take time off for union work under the existing facilities agreement. There was also the union-related factor of the process of shop steward recruitment inasmuch as proportionately more men than women had been asked by work colleagues to stand for election as shop steward. In addition, an unfavourable management response to union activism on the part of female workers may have been a factor. Under-representation at branch committee level and at branch officer level and above may have been related to the timing of meetings in evenings and at weekends. The NALGO branch had attempted to address these problems by providing assistance with childcare and by seeking to negotiate cover for union work.

Once elected as shop steward, men and women did not exhibit major differences in attitudes towards union office-holding. Their experience as shop steward was, however, influenced by their occupational position. This was most noticeable in the operation of the union facilities agreement. Women stewards were using considerably more of their own time to do NALGO work than were men. While this can be explained to a large degree in terms of occupational status, the interviews suggested that gender role factors were also relevant. Both male and female interviewees reported that women were more likely than men to try to make up work lost because of time taken out for union work. This suggests that the operation of union facility agreements is an important area for trade unions to consider when seeking to increase women's representation in union office-holding.

There were no significant differences found in willingness to take industrial action nor in the extent of action taken by each sex. The one gender difference found in experiences of industrial action was that some groups of women, such as the nursery nurses, had found gender role characteristics used against them when taking industrial action.

There were no gender differences in shop steward turnover rates, despite the fact that the union facilities agreement worked better for men than for women. Interview material did suggest, however, that there were some gender differences in reasons for turnover. Male shop stewards were more likely to be promoted and so to resign from union office. Female shop stewards were more likely to stand down because of the pressures of their work and the lack of cover of their jobs when doing union work. The pressures and stresses of union work were, however, felt substantially by both sexes, especially at the branch officer level.

Lay activists play a vital role in maintaining trade unions as democratic organizations. An adequate level of representation of all groups of members is also an important aspect of union democracy. The impact of feminism on trade unions has contributed towards increasing female representation and to the strengthening of unions as collective organizations. NALGO was a union with a strong tradition of local lay officers running the union at a day-to-day level. This helped to make the union democratic, but it also placed substantial personal demands on the lay activists in terms of both their time and the stresses arising from the responsibilities they undertook. Hence the importance, which was widely recognized by informants, of time off and cover for union work.

Chapter 6

Gender, Collective Bargaining and Union Policy Issues

Introduction

In the previous chapter gender and unions have been examined in terms of issues of participation and representation. This chapter will consider the related aspect of union policies. The impact of feminism on the trade union movement in the 1970s and 1980s led to demands both for better representation of women in unions and for changes in union policies to give greater support to women's rights. These policy developments in the unions have been discussed in Chapter 2. The research explored the extent to which these changes in union policies had affected the union at branch level. This was investigated in the questionnaire with questions about bargaining priorities and views of women's position in society. In the interviews, questions were asked about NALGO's equal opportunities work and about gender issues in collective bargaining.

The material in this chapter is organized in the following sections: gender differences in collective bargaining; union policy on sexual harassment; shop stewards' awareness of gender inequality in society; and NALGO's policies on equal rights.

Gender Differences in Collective Bargaining

Three related themes concerning gender differences in collective bargaining will be discussed: priorities for bargaining; styles of bargaining; and gender issues in collective bargaining.

Collective bargaining is arguably the most important activity of a trade union. Members in the Sheffield NALGO Local Government Branch were affected by three levels of bargaining: national, branch and departmental. In some departments, departmental level bargaining was conducted almost entirely by the shop stewards' committee; in other departments, branch officers were likely to be involved at an earlier stage.

Gender differences in collective bargaining may take the form of both differences in priorities for bargaining and differences in styles of bargaining. So far, research on gender and unions has not established definitively whether there are gender differences in these areas. Unions have at times taken up issues of equal rights in collective bargaining and this work has increased to some extent as a result of the impact of second-wave feminism on trade unions. The degree to which this had happened in the Sheffield NALGO Local Government Branch will be discussed later in this chapter.

Priorities for Bargaining

Effective trade union organization involves identifying priorities for bargaining and campaigning which can mobilize and unify the membership. It is not, however, always easy for unions as collective organizations to identify what their members' priorities are. Members may have different priorities arising from their work situations. It is also possible, although it has not been proved, that male and female members have different bargaining priorities. The traditional trade union stereotypes have often assumed that men are more interested in money and women in conditions of work, shorter working hours and holidays. These stereotypes are related to assumptions that men are breadwinners and women are primarily homemakers. The problem with these assumptions is that they are not based on careful research, they tend to ignore occupational divisions within each sex, and they ignore variations in personal and family circumstances. Moreover, the assumption that women are less interested in pay than men makes little logical sense when one considers the fact that women are paid less than men and so have more material interest in higher pay as a bargaining priority than men. Indeed, as will be seen in discussing the questionnaire findings, tackling the problem of low pay was seen as a bargaining priority for women. It was, however, strongly supported by shop stewards of both sexes. This illustrates the difficulty of identifying issues on the trade union bargaining agenda as exclusively 'men's issues' or 'women's issues'. Many bargaining achievements may disproportionately benefit one sex, but still benefit both sexes: these include obtaining a workplace nursery or an agreement on personal leave. Moreover, trade unions as collective organizations are based on recognition of the common interests of all workers, as expressed in the

Table 6.1: Views of NALGO's Negotiating Priorities — Male Shop Stewards

Negotiating Priority	Value of Ranking		
	First Ranking	Second Ranking	Third Ranking
Service conditions	23.8%	16.7%	9.5%
Higher pay	16.7%	16.7%	11.9%
Equal opportunities	4.8%	9.5%	9.5%
Shorter working week	4.8%	4.8%	9.5%
Health and safety	0.0%	11.9%	26.2%
More time off for trade union work	2.4%	0.0%	0.0%
New technology agreements	0.0%	0.0%	0.0%
Pay increases for the lower paid	31.0%	16.7%	11.9%
Job security	9.5%	16.7%	11.9%
More opportunities for training and promotion	2.4%	2.4%	2.4%
Workplace nursery	0.0%	2.4%	7.1%

slogan, 'an injury to one is an injury to all — a victory for one is a victory for all'.

From this perspective of trade unionism, at the end of the day, there are no distinct sectional interests whether based on occupation, gender or any other division. Arguments about trade union solidarity can be used by radicals in the labour movement to argue that affirmative action is in the interests of white males, or can be used by conservatives to argue that women and black people are being divisive when they demand that the labour movement supports action to end discrimination. Thus trade union unity does not rest upon ignoring inequalities among workers. It involves a balancing act between finding demands and campaigns which can easily unify the whole membership and supporting the demands of groups of workers who have been disadvantaged and discriminated against. To achieve this balance, unions need to identify the bargaining priorities of their membership.

In the questionnaire stage of the research, informants were asked a rank order question about their views of what NALGO's bargaining priorities should be. The answers of male and female shop stewards are shown in tables 6.1 and 6.2. The most popular bargaining priority for both sexes was 'pay increases for the lower paid'. Twenty-three shop stewards (35.9 per cent) put this first. The second most popular priority was 'service conditions' which was put first by fifteen shop stewards (23.4 per cent). For male shop stewards the two clear bargaining priorities were 'pay increases for the lower paid' and 'service conditions'. Their third priority was 'higher pay'.

Table 6.2: *Views of NALGO's Negotiating Priorities — Female Shop Stewards*

Negotiating Priority	Value of Ranking		
	First Ranking	Second Ranking	Third Ranking
Service conditions	22.7%	9.1%	27.3%
Higher pay	0.0%	18.2%	9.1%
Equal opportunities	9.1%	4.5%	4.5%
Shorter working week	0.0%	4.5%	4.5%
Health and safety	0.0%	13.6%	9.1%
More time off for trade union work	0.0%	0.0%	4.5%
New technology agreements	4.5%	4.5%	9.1%
Pay increases for the lower paid	45.5%	27.3%	4.5%
Job security	9.1%	0.0%	4.5%
More opportunities for training and promotion	4.5%	13.6%	13.6%
Workplace nursery	0.0%	0.0%	9.1%

Female shop stewards shared the two most popular bargaining priorities with their male colleagues. Indeed, female shop stewards demonstrated a stronger level of support for these demands: 45.5 per cent of the women and 31.0 per cent of the men put 'pay increases for the lower paid' first, and 22.7 per cent of the women and 23.8 per cent of the men put 'service conditions' first. Men did attach more importance to 'higher pay' than women, with seven men (16.7 per cent) ranking this first, whereas no women did. Women did rate 'new technology agreements' and 'more opportunities for training and promotion' more highly than men. It is reasonable to assume that this reflected their occupational experience in council employment.

The questionnaire results suggest that there are some gender differences in bargaining priorities, but that the similarities are greater. Many interviewees seemed to share this view. The most frequently mentioned difference in bargaining issues related to negotiating policies on dealing with sexual harassment. The following reply is typical of the responses:

Well there's the issue of sexual harassment. But I don't think there are many differences on other issues, but of course low pay affects women more than men, but it's not exclusive to women. (Female shop steward)

Another negotiating issue mentioned by one male shop steward which particularly affected women was new technology. He noted that female workers tended to use word-processors for longer periods than men and that often the word-processors were badly positioned in terms of safety. Another male shop steward was aware of women in his department raising the issue of time off to look after sick children. The branch organizer stated that women members had raised with her the issue of childcare provision by the employer after the Midland Bank had announced the provision of childcare for its employees.

One interviewee explained the difficulty of distinguishing different priorities related to grade and to gender:

> I can't think of any differences between men and women in a particular area that I have dealt with. There are differences between areas, but the department tends to be organized so that one particular job is perceived as a women's job, therefore there are very few men in it. Similarly on the technician side they are nearly all males. There are tensions between groups but I can't really say that's necessarily down to gender. (Male chief shop steward)

Another interviewee mentioned the job-sharing issue, which had been seen in the branch as a priority for women, although in fact it was an issue for all members.

> *So do you think women members have different priorities sometimes for the issues the union should be taking up in collective bargaining?*
> Yes, yes certainly, yes, I mean job-sharing was definitely seen as a woman's issue within this branch and as a women's priority. It isn't, but that's how women saw it at the time, and women pushed that along. (Female branch officer)

The final part of this statement indicates a strong recognition by senior women activists in the branch that most issues affected both sexes, as illustrated in the following observation from a female shop steward.

> The low pay thing at the end of the day is about pay, and while there's many more women that fall into the low-pay category, it's not an exclusive women's thing. An evening up of pay is seen as important by a lot of members.

The female branch organizer had found male and female members equally supportive of NALGO's campaign against low pay in local government, although a majority of the low-paid members were female. She stated:

> In my experience it's just as likely to be the 'higher-paid' male shop stewards speaking on behalf of the low-paid women workers as it is to be a woman. It isn't out of any sense of 'I'm doing the right thing'. It's because they have recognized that the issue is a trade union issue, it's not just an issue for women.

This sense of issues being recognized as trade union issues and so as issues for all members could also be applied to the issue of sexual harassment. The branch organizer argued that this was a union issue for all members, but that it was one in which women's views needed to be taken especially into account. So the gender distinction that operated here was not that it was an issue only for women members, but that it was an issue in which women needed to take the lead in policy-making.

> There are issues on which a branch should take the views of women into account. If you're talking about sexual harassment, I wouldn't expect, nor would it happen that men would make decisions without actually taking the views of women on board, but that doesn't make it a women's issue. In terms of moving forward I think it is divisive to say 'these are women's issues' because we could say 'well, those are men's issues' and leave it to men to deal with them, or 'these are black members' issues', but they're all our issues. Apartheid isn't an issue only for black members, it's an issue for white members as well. (Female branch organizer)

To some degree this similarity in bargaining priorities between male and female trade unionists may reflect a degree of similarity in lifestyle, in that both groups were in most cases in full-time employment. One senior female activist, who had served in the past as branch equal opportunities officer, pointed out that trade unions need to consider not only inequalities in work, but inequalities in being able to get to work in the first place. She referred to the problems of people with disabilities, women with young children and women returners in obtaining employment.

> I think people do have different priorities, but sometimes I think that the priorities that people have determine whether or

not they are actually able to come to work at all. (Female shop steward)

Styles of Bargaining

Some interviewees commented that while they were not necessarily aware of gender differences in priorities for bargaining, they did believe that men and women sometimes used different styles of bargaining and approached it in a different way.

> I certainly think there are different styles of bargaining. However right-on the men may be, sometimes they do find it, and I include myself in this, very difficult not to be putting a forthright and strident and traditional macho position to management. Women are less likely to do that. That certainly is a distinction that I'm conscious of. (Male shop steward, F&CS)

He noted, too, that when he had employed a less macho style of bargaining, Personnel staff who had expected an antagonistic session had been really surprised to find him so reasonable.

An example of an effective low-key style of bargaining was given by one of the branch organizers:

> I've always worked on the basis that if I can achieve what I've set out to achieve, on behalf of whoever I'm representing, by persuading the people across the table from me that it was their idea in the first place and they can take the credit for it, then that's fine by me. But the men I've worked with don't like working like that. They want to be the ones to say 'we've negotiated this, I've got this for my members'. (Female branch organizer)

She stressed, too, that negotiating is a learned skill, and that while not every shop steward might be good at it, both men and women can learn bargaining skills. This sort of approach to bargaining demystifies it as an activity and removes it from being associated with any innate characteristics of people. One of the difficulties about learning bargaining skills is obtaining the necessary experience of bargaining. Given the important issues for the members often involved in bargaining, experienced negotiators sometimes found it difficult to let newer and less experienced stewards take the lead in negotiations. Here there was a possible conflict between the short-term interest of the union, to have the best possible negotiator, and the long-term interest, to develop more shop stewards with negotiating skills.

> When you know that you can do something, and you're with another steward and you're not sure whether they can do it or not, giving them the space to negotiate, and potentially not do it as well as you would, is always difficult, but I think that's something you've got to overcome. I wouldn't have got on as far as I did if people hadn't allowed me to do negotiating and make mistakes. (Female shop steward)

The opportunity for new stewards to develop negotiating skills was important in encouraging women's representation in the union. The following statement by one of the female branch officers emphasizes the importance of women being involved in negotiations, on grounds both of different perspectives on negotiations and different negotiating styles.

> *So you said you were involved with the local negotiating committee as a branch officer. Do you think it's important for women to get involved in negotiating work?*
> Yes, very much so, to put the woman's point of view, because I do believe that women have a different perspective on how things should be done. I do believe that men and women are equal, but I also believe that women function in a different way. I think that women come at it from a very different angle, I mean I don't think that we are aggressive about how we negotiate in this branch, because that isn't how we do it, but I do think women come from a slightly different angle when they're negotiating. (Female branch officer)

On the other hand, another female steward discussed the importance of resisting gender stereotypes in bargaining. Where there was a substantial number of women shop stewards in a department they had been able to work out strategies to do this, but gender roles tended to be re-asserted when women were negotiating alongside men.

> *Are there sometimes different styles of bargaining of men and women?*
> I think there are different styles of bargaining first. I'm sure the differences do show themselves in women and men. When

I was first active as a shop steward a lot of the work I did was with other women shop stewards. We used to talk sometimes about who was going to take the dominant role. We'd use the classic set-up. One of us goes in screaming and shouting and the other comes in all calm and reasonable. When there are two women doing it you can swap the roles. I think there is an issue about men automatically adopting the dominant role. It is more difficult for women to lead in negotiations with men. (Female shop steward)

Taking up Gender Issues in Collective Bargaining

Trade unions can take up gender issues in collective bargaining both by placing items of specific concern to women members on the agenda and by promoting women as negotiators. To some degree both processes were happening in the Sheffield NALGO Local Government Branch. As recounted in relation to the new technology dispute and regrading disputes, the branch and departmental shop stewards' committees had put a lot of energy into particular campaigns which concerned low-paid women members.

Agreements had been negotiated on areas like job-sharing, working with new technology and career progression for low-paid workers (the clerical career grade). The branch had not been successful, despite attempts to do so, in negotiating for the provision of a workplace nursery. Nonetheless the negotiating priorities which had been taken up by the branch and by departmental shop stewards' committees had not been ones which neglected the interests of women members.

There had also been attempts, particularly at departmental level, to encourage union office-holding by women. In well organized departments, efforts had also been made to negotiate cover for shop stewards, which would have particularly assisted lower-status women workers to take on union office and hence participate in collective bargaining.

Union Policy on Sexual Harassment

Negotiating to protect members facing sexual harassment was identified by some interviewees as a bargaining priority for women. At a national level NALGO had issued publicity material about sexual harassment and campaigned against it. The early stages of trade union policy on sexual harassment had involved both educating female members that they had a right to object to offensive behaviour and educating male members about what forms of behaviour constituted harassment and were unacceptable. One of the branch officers described this process.

> *Are members getting more politicized on the issue of sexual harassment?*
> Yes, I think so, because we have been doing a lot of work around it, so women are beginning to understand it much more and I think so are men, but I think there is still a long, long way to go dealing with that. It's very subtle, sexual harassment can be very subtle and because of the position of women in society anyway women are loth to put that name to it. (Female branch officer)

At the time of the research there was a debate going on in the branch about how to handle cases of harassment. Some aspects of this had been fairly straightforward, such as the recognition that women with complaints of harassment needed female officers and stewards to handle their cases. In the case of black members complaining of racist harassment, NALGO tried to find a black representative to assist them.

> We do try, if it's a woman who's suffering from sexual harassment then it is a woman steward or a woman branch officer who deals with it, if it's racial harassment we find a black steward or a black member who will help that person. (Female branch officer)

One of the most difficult issues for unions in dealing with harassment cases is the problem of representing both sides if the complainant and the alleged harasser are both members of the union. This issue was very much at the sharp end of equal opportunities policy. The branch organizer explained that there were two trains of thought about this debate. One view was that all members were entitled to representation. The other view was that there were some circumstances in which unions should not represent members. This latter view had been adopted by the shop stewards' committee in Family and Community Services after much debate.

> We've taken a position of non-representation of people accused of harassment. That is a very hard position that people find

> difficult to understand, but there again I think that is being more honest and is actually being more up-front about what is at the heart of equal opportunities policies. What you are talking about is empowering people who have less power than those who exercise it most of the time. (Male shop steward, F&CS)

There were some reservations about the F&CS position within the branch. The consequence of the departmental shop stewards' committee not representing the alleged harasser could mean that representation was provided by branch or district levels of the union. This could, one branch officer suggested, actually advantage the alleged harasser, since a branch or district NALGO representative might have more credibility with the management than a departmental representative.

> There are more complex issues about representation that we've not sorted out in the branch, particularly I'm thinking about areas like sexual harassment. Historically the branch has had a view that it represents everybody, so if you have a member who is making an accusation of sexual harassment against another NALGO member, we finish up representing both or ought to in some people's eyes. Now I've every confidence in the stewards in F&CS, but given management's response and attitudes to power relationships, I'd be worried, because if a branch or district officer were representing the person accused, the management might give more weight towards that person, in the case of branch officers because they deal with us frequently and in the case of district officers because of their status. I don't want to be in that sort of situation. So there are some of us in the middle of the debate who are saying we've got to have a mechanism where there's automatic representation for the person making an accusation, but the person who is being accused has got to justify the right of representation from the union. (Male branch officer)

What the debate about representation in cases of harassment shows is that the branch had been able to respond to new issues. The educational work of explaining to members what is meant by sexual harassment had been tackled. There was also a recognition that changing people's behaviour in this area was a long-term task. There had been a willingness to rethink traditional policy about representing all members, and whether it was appropriate over this issue, although different conclusions had been reached about it.

Clearly the comments in interviews showed that there had been consciousness-raising about the problem of sexual harassment and extensive discussion about how to deal with it. It was still an on-going debate inasmuch as there was no easy answer to the problem of representation in harassment cases. This arises partly because the facts of the matter may be in dispute. It may not be until well into the hearing of the case that it is possible to establish definitely whether harassment has occurred or not. Moreover, if the union conducts some sort of internal enquiry before granting representation this could be seen as prejudging the issue before the employer hears the complaint. This is the difficulty with the position of asking members to justify their right of representation. Nonetheless, unions cannot represent members clearly guilty of harassment, if that representation is taken to implicitly exonerate such conduct or minimize its seriousness. Thus unions face a conflict between the rights of members to representation, which includes the right to be presumed innocent until proven guilty, and their commitment to fighting sexism and racism, which includes finding ways of empowering women and black members.

Shop Stewards' Awareness of Gender Inequality in Society

As the previous section on sexual harassment indicates, there had been considerable discussion in the branch about some aspects of women's oppression. Shop stewards' awareness of gender inequalities in relation to employment and union work has been discussed earlier in the book, especially in relation to union office-holding and facility time. Their awareness of gender inequality at a societal level was explored with an attitudinal question in the questionnaire.

The statements were designed to test support for women's rights and views of the position of men and women over a number of issues. Some of these statements were ones where a clear feminist position might be identified, such as support for women's right to work, women's right to choose abortion, and nursery provision. Other statements were less obviously related to demands of the women's movement and were designed to test how deeply informants had thought about gender roles and women's position in society. They thus addressed issues debated among supporters of women's rights. These included whether the Equal Pay Act and Sex Discrimination Act had improved women's position, whether men are as oppressed by gender roles as women, and whether women fail to take up opportunities for equal representation in public life. This last question was included to assess whether there was any support for a more conservative and individualistic view of equal opportunities, which sees women as partly to blame for continuing inequality.

Some of these answers, as shown in table 6.3, showed very low levels of gender difference. The question about whether equal rights legislation had done much to improve the position of women produced a scattered response for both sexes. A critical view of the legislation was demonstrated by 50 per cent of the woman and 42.9 per cent of the men. No one opposed the statement that 'all women should have the right to seek paid work'. The principle of women's right to paid employment was strongly supported by both male and female stewards, if rather more strongly by women: 72.7 per cent of the women and 61.9 per cent of the men strongly agreed with this statement. There was no support for the traditional view that women's place is in the home.

The next statement, 'men are oppressed by sex roles as much as women are', was a statement which produced a scattered response among both sexes. Half the women and a third of the men disagreed with this statement, giving the conventional feminist response. Support for nursery provision for all children under five was overwhelming among both sexes: 95.2 per cent of the male stewards and 90.9 per cent of the female stewards agreed with the statement 'nurseries should be available for all children under five'. This shows widespread acceptance of one of the demands of the women's movement. NALGO has done a certain amount of campaigning for workplace nursery provision, which may have influenced informants' views.

Support for positive action policies to give women equality at work was strong: 81.8 per cent of the women and 83.3 per cent of the men agreed with the need for such policies. As with the case of nursery provision this indicates support for NALGO's policies on equal rights. Belief in the maternal instinct, as expressed in the statement 'women instinctively care for children better than men do' was strongly rejected by both sexes: 57.1 per cent of the men and 68.2 per cent of the women disagreed with this statement.

Recognition of continuing inequalities between men and women was strongly evidenced by both male and female shop stewards. The statement 'women still experience discrimination and unequal treatment in many aspects of life' was strongly supported by both sexes, with

Table 6.3: *Shop Stewards' Views of Gender Inequality in Society*

	Strongly Agree	Agree	Undecided	Disagree	Strongly Disagree
The Equal Pay Act and Sex Discrimination Act have done much to improve the position of women.					
Male Stewards	0.0%	40.5%	16.7%	38.1%	4.8%
Female Stewards	9.1%	27.3%	13.6%	50.0%	0.0%
All women should have the right to seek paid work.					
Male Stewards	61.9%	38.1%	0.0%	0.0%	0.0%
Female Stewards	72.7%	22.7%	4.5%	0.0%	0.0%
Men are oppressed by sex roles as much as women are.					
Male Stewards	19.0%	31.0%	16.7%	26.2%	7.1%
Female Stewards	9.1%	36.4%	4.5%	40.9%	9.1%
Nurseries should be available for all children under five.					
Male Stewards	59.5%	35.7%	2.4%	0.0%	0.0%
Female Stewards	63.6%	27.3%	4.5%	4.5%	0.0%
Positive action policies are needed to give women real equality at work.					
Male Stewards	38.1%	45.2%	2.4%	11.9%	2.4%
Female Stewards	45.5%	36.4%	4.5%	13.6%	0.0%
Women instinctively care for children better than men do.					
Male Stewards	2.4%	19.0%	19.0%	45.2%	11.9%
Female Stewards	9.1%	9.1%	13.6%	45.5%	22.7%
Women still experience discrimination and unequal treatment in many aspects of life.					
Male Stewards	50.0%	47.6%	0.0%	2.4%	0.0%
Female Stewards	54.5%	36.4%	9.1%	0.0%	0.0%
Women should have the right to choose whether to have an abortion.					
Male Stewards	66.7%	28.6%	4.8%	0.0%	0.0%
Female Stewards	45.5%	27.3%	13.6%	9.1%	4.5%
Women often fail to take up opportunities for equal representation in public life.					
Male Stewards	11.9%	50.0%	11.9%	19.0%	4.8%
Female Stewards	31.8%	54.5%	13.6%	0.0%	0.0%
Laws on social security and taxation should be changed to treat men and women equally.					
Male Stewards	66.7%	26.2%	2.4%	2.4%	0.0%
Female Stewards	77.3%	22.7%	0.0%	0.0%	0.0%

97.6 per cent of the male stewards and 90.9 per cent of the female stewards agreeing. This suggests that, while there was a mixed response to the issue of how effective equal rights legislation had been, there was an understanding that equality has not yet been achieved.

Support for women's abortion rights was stronger among male stewards than female stewards, with 66.7 per cent of the men and 45.5 per cent of the women strongly agreeing with the statement 'women should have the right to choose whether to have an abortion'. Abortion rights has always been one of the most controversial aspects of unions' women's rights policies. It was an issue on which NALGO as a union nationally had taken a clear pro-choice stand.

The statement 'women often fail to take up opportunities for equal representation in public life' was slightly more strongly supported by women than men. A majority of stewards of both sexes agreed with it. This implies that they thought that to some degree the responsibility for under-representation lay with women. This question was asked at a time when there was a woman prime minister and a certain amount of political propaganda arguing that opportunities were there for women if only they would take them up. Maybe, too, shop stewards, because they had taken on representative office themselves, were less sympathetic to others who were more reluctant to do so.

Support for changes in social security and taxation law to treat men and women equally was given by both sexes. All the women and 92.9 per cent of the men agreed that such changes should take place.

What these answers show overall is considerable support among shop stewards of both sexes for women's rights. This may indicate that NALGO's policies were representative of their active membership and that shop stewards had been influenced by union policies in support of equal rights. The gender differences in replies were not substantial. On five statements women gave more feminist replies than men. These were 'all women should have the right to seek paid work'; 'men are oppressed by sex roles as much as women are'; 'positive action policies are needed to give women real equality at work'; 'women instinctively care for children better than men do'; and 'laws on social security and taxation should be changed to treat men and women equally'. On two statements men gave more feminist replies than women. These were 'women should have the right to choose whether to have an abortion' and 'women often fail to take up opportunities for equal representation in public life'.

Comments in interviews gave further indications of levels of understanding of equal rights. Awareness of the processes of gender inequalities in employment was illustrated in a number of comments.

One informant noted that men tended to plan their careers more than women did:

> I think there's a difference between men and women regarding careers. I think men enter into thinking about careers as an essential thing in their early twenties. That's partly that they are forced into it, partly they choose it because they are looking for promotions. (Female shop steward)

Another interviewee commented on the lack of women applicants when the Director of Libraries post became available. She did not explain this in terms of women's failure to apply, but in terms of the failure of the Library Department to provide career development for women.

> Libraries is a traditionally low-paid women's department where there is a very great distinction between professional and non-professional grades. The thing that staggered me in Libraries is that when the director left, they didn't get a single woman applicant for Director of Libraries, although there was a national advertisement. In a service that's got the highest proportion of women, there was not a single woman applicant for the chief officer post. That's got to say a lot about the way the department fails to encourage women to look for careers. (Female shop steward)

In one department a male NALGO shop steward had campaigned successfully to improve equal opportunities. His shop stewards' committee had been in favour of all posts being internally advertised first, which conflicted with equal opportunities, because it meant that groups currently under-represented in employment would stay under-represented. As he notes, the departmental policy was against branch policy, and this may have made it easier to overturn it.

> Up until three years ago our shop stewards' committee had a policy of internal advertisement first, which was against branch policy. I promoted a campaign to change that to concurrent advertising. I wasn't chief shop steward at the time. The chief shop steward opposed that, being a fairly old male technician. We held general meetings through the department and my view won the day, so that perhaps proves our members do support equal opportunities. (Male chief shop steward)

A couple of interviewees mentioned the issue of ring-fencing when a redeployment process was taking place. This presents difficulties for unions, and for employers with a genuine commitment to equal opportunities, because there is a responsibility to protect the employment of existing staff, but this delays increasing the proportion of under-represented groups in the organization. This type of issue indicates the problems for trade unions of how equal rights policies are implemented in practice. This difficulty was expressed in the two following statements in reply to questions about how much support there was among members for NALGO's equal opportunities policies.

> In terms of the issues of equal opportunities, yes there is an awareness, but what we haven't grasped is how to deal with them in practical terms. (Female branch organizer)

> *How much support is there among members for NALGO's policies on equal opportunities?*
> I think there's total support theoretically, but when you ask people what they are going to do about it, then that's the problem. A lot of people see these issues as work issues rather than union issues. (Male shop steward)

Understanding of how women's position in society can affect their situation in trade unions was shown in the following statements from male shop stewards.

> On our shop stewards' committee the nursery officers rarely contribute to the discussion, unless it's about their service. When it's about their service they are very confident. They rarely get involved in discussion about general issues. (Male shop steward)

> Trade unions have until recently been a man's world and although some progress has been made towards breaking that down, we've got a long way to go. One of our shop stewards, who's been active a long time, fifteen years ago she got wolf whistles as she walked to the platform to speak at conference. (Male chief shop steward)

One of the women branch officers, however, also indicated the positive ways in which women's experiences of discrimination can be used in trade unions to support other oppressed groups.

Women I find tend to understand more of the issues around racism, but that's partly because they are a group of people who are discriminated against as well. (Female branch officer)

NALGO's Policies on Equal Rights

Actions taken by unions nationally to raise women's levels of union representation and develop policies on women's rights have been discussed in Chapter 2. These developments had also taken place at the local level within the Sheffield NALGO Local Government Branch. One of the practical aspects of this was to include the issue in shop stewards' training. The education officer explained in interview how one way the NALGO branch had expressed its commitment to equal opportunities was to make it a compulsory item in shop stewards' training.

> There is a slot on equal opportunities on branch training. That is formal branch policy. On union training courses students are allowed to set their own agenda, but it must include something on women and something on race. Sexual harassment is always chosen by women as an issue.

The branch had an equal opportunities sub-committee which was responsible for the day-to-day development of equal opportunities work. This work had been organized in a number of ways. Sometimes well-attended and successful meetings of members had been organized on issues such as job-sharing and the positive action project. At first the equal opportunities sub-committee had been composed of the equal opportunities officer, the two service conditions officers, the branch organizer and any members who cared to attend. The problem with this very open structure was that the committee had been unable to develop any coherent long-term priorities for its work, since different members would attend each meeting and raise different issues.

Moreover there was a danger of the equal opportunities committee becoming a dumping ground for many equal opportunities issues which should have been addressed elsewhere in the branch. One of the ex-equal opportunities officers described the problem as follows:

> The equal opportunities committee and the equal opportunities officer had become a dumping ground for things that nobody else quite knew what to do with. It was also a

conscience-salve. 'We've got an equal opportunities committee, give it to them to deal with.' There was no recognition
within the mainstream of the branch that equality issues affected them. So you'd have a service conditions committee
meeting once a month, and all they did with issues relating to
women, black people and disability was to pass them to the
equal opportunities committee to deal with. It just became
marginalized to the extent that as Equal Opportunities Officer,
I used to get all the post that came from CND. That really is
an equal opportunities issue! (Female ex-equal opportunities
officer)

As this statement shows, an equal opportunities committee can
easily become overloaded not only because work is passed on from
other committees, but also because it is trying to tackle all forms of
discrimination simultaneously. Following these early problems in the
organization of equal opportunities work, the branch was reorganizing
its equal opportunities work. The proposed reorganization was similar
to that adopted by NALGO nationally with four self-organizing groups,
one for women members, one for gay and lesbian members, one for
black members and one for members with disabilities. The purpose of
this reorganization was both to create space for disadvantaged groups
to articulate their demands and to give some stability and focus to this
work.

One interesting and significant aspect of the way equal rights
work in relation to women had been conducted was that there was an
understanding of occupational divisions among women. The senior
female activists leading this work did not assume that all women had
exactly the same interests or would be mobilized on the same issues.
They were very conscious of the danger of feminism being seen as a
middle-class women's issue. In terms of feminist politics they were
operating within a framework which recognized diversity among women
and believed that this needed to be acknowledged and incorporated
into union organizing strategies. The organization of assertiveness
training courses, for instance, had been undertaken to challenge inequalities of both gender and class. Attempts to negotiate provision of
a workplace nursery had raised income differences among women in
a sharp way. The council had been prepared to provide a nursery, but
the proposed charges were more than most women in council employment could afford. The result was that the branch had opposed
nursery provision on the basis on which the council was offering it.

We'd almost reached agreement on getting a workplace nursery introduced in the council, and some of the women within
the branch actually got it thrown out, because the charges were
way beyond the financial capacity of most women who worked
for the council. It wasn't a nursery for other than reasonably
well-paid women. (Female shop steward)

The existence of these social divisions among women was also
illustrated by an incident recounted by one of the equal opportunities
officers I interviewed. The equal opportunities committee decided to
organize a women-only social event for the women shop stewards.
Only four women shop stewards attended. Women-only socials were
clearly seen as a 'middle-class feminist' scene. As she put it:

Many women stewards did not see the point of a women-only
gathering. (Female equal opportunities officer)

Another female equal opportunities officer discussed differences among
women in terms of personal situation, occupation and education.

Higher-paid women have better access to childcare facilities.
Women who have husbands with a decent income might feel
they have a choice about whether to work when they have
children. Women who are in poorer families or who haven't
got the support of a partner who is earning, might not have a
choice about whether they return to work, and I think there is
a social class issue. In terms of educational background as well,
people have different expectations and ambitions for themselves. Whilst I think there's a difference in ambition between
men and women, I think there's a difference between different
women, who've been through different life experiences. I'm
seen as an educated person, who's managed to progress into a
reasonably well-paid job. What credibility am I going to have
with people who are still low-paid and at the bottom of the
ladder? I think traditionally feminism has been seen as a middle-
class issue, and that's very much to do with being educated and
articulate.

One way the branch had tried to tackle the issue of being able to
articulate grievances and demands was to provide assertiveness training. The branch education officer reported that she was organizing

assertiveness training for women shop stewards. This was aimed to
tackle inequalities of both gender and class.

> I'm trying to organize assertiveness training for women shop
> stewards, a stage beyond women's bridging courses, particu-
> larly for women in low-paid jobs from local backgrounds. These
> lower-paid women tend to be suspicious of 'middle-class femi-
> nists'. (Female branch officer)

This work was later continued by another female branch officer.
It was not only aimed at women shop stewards, but was potentially
for all women members. The purpose of the course was not only to
develop women as union activists, but to help them to become more
assertive generally. Thus the focus was on changing women's situation
in work and in their personal lives, as well as enabling them to be
more assertive about raising women's issues in the union. These courses
were being organized both in Sheffield and on a district basis.

> *What's the take-up been for those courses?*
> Well I ran them. I've run four courses, two for Sheffield branch
> which were for nursery nurses. We did them primarily for
> nursery nurses at the end of the dispute. You can only deal
> with twelve, thirteen people on any course and they were full
> and we ran two district courses both of which have been full
> and we're running another one in January. It is an on-going
> process and the women enjoy it. We have recall days where
> they can get together and it acts as a support for women as
> well, so the women in Sheffield had got immediate support,
> the women in the district tend to keep a network going so they
> know other women.
> *And at those recall days what was the feedback, had it empow-
> ered the women?*
> Yes, on the recall day that we have just done a fortnight ago,
> three of the women in the group had changed their jobs and
> two had left their husbands. It certainly empowered them to
> take decisions that they had been wanting to take for some
> considerable time. They had all felt better able to go back to
> their jobs and to state what they wanted. They all said that
> they had learned to say no which was very effective, because
> women at the bottom of the pecking order tend to get work

piled on them and they'd learned to say no, they couldn't do
any more. (Female branch officer)

Conclusion

The research on collective bargaining and union work on equal rights
undertaken in this study indicates both gender differences and also
areas where male and female stewards had similar priorities. In terms
of priorities for collective bargaining both male and female stewards
had the same main priorities, namely improving pay of lower-paid
workers and protecting and improving service conditions. There was
some gender variation in other bargaining priorities, with men focusing
more on higher pay and women being more concerned about new
technology and training and promotion. These gender differences can
be related to employment position. Overall, however, the research
findings do not support the view that there is a big gender gap in
bargaining priorities.

Some gender differences were found in styles of collective bargaining, with women tending to adopt a more low-key style of bargaining. These differences arose both from gender roles of shop
stewards and from attitudes of some male managers, who did not feel
comfortable negotiating with women. Where a number of women were
involved in bargaining on a team, they had tried to develop strategies
to break down these gender roles. Gender differences were clearly
stronger in styles of bargaining than in priorities for bargaining.

Issues of gender inequality had been addressed by the branch in
a number of areas of collective bargaining. These were regrading of
lower-paid, mainly female, staff, such as nursery nurses; nursery
provision; use of new technology; and cover for shop stewards. It
appears, therefore, that union policy on equal rights had had some
impact on the branch's negotiating priorities, despite the problems of
organization of equal opportunities work.

Questions on gender roles in society showed that support for
equal rights was strong among shop stewards of both sexes. The
similarities between women and men were greater here than the
differences. This may be the result of working in a local government
culture, with a strong formal commitment to equal opportunities. It
may also reflect the influence of trade union education on these issues.

Attempts to develop equal opportunities work at branch level
had encountered a number of problems and the branch had rethought

ways of organizing on these issues. Interviews showed an ability to be self-critical and to avoid complacency about what the branch was doing in this area. Among the officers involved in this work there was an understanding of the complexity and diversity of equal opportunities issues. Despite the problems of branch organization in terms of finding the right structures for equal opportunities work, innovative work had been carried out around assertiveness training, which had been able to address inequalities of both gender and class.

Chapter 7

Conclusion

The conclusion will first summarize the main results of the research and then discuss its policy implications. The examination of approaches to union participation showed that researchers have in the past often looked at reasons for union participation in the case of men and obstacles to union participation in the case of women. Thus a different problem for sociological explanation was identified according to the sex of the workers being studied. This may indicate a serious flaw in research strategy, which a feminist perspective should correct. The study of union participation should not start from an assumption that women always have lower levels of union participation than men, and should avoid the twin dangers of ignoring the influence of men's gender roles and women's work roles on union participation (Feldberg and Glenn, 1979).

The study of Sheffield NALGO attempted to build on past studies of women's union participation without starting from an assumption that women have lower levels of participation than men or tend 'naturally' to be less active in unions. Even if this approach may have been justified in the past, it can be argued that in the context of changes in women's position in trade unions in the 1980s it is no longer appropriate. It should always be kept in mind that union activism, outside exceptional periods, is a minority activity for both male and female workers. The categories of work-related, societal-cultural-personal and union-related which Wertheimer and Nelson (1975) proposed for the investigation of barriers to union participation have been employed in this study to examine reasons for participation as well as obstacles to it. An adequate sociological explanation of union participation needs to encompass reasons for participation as well as obstacles to participation. Tackling barriers to participation, such as responsibility for housework and childcare or requirements to work overtime, is necessary as part of a union strategy to increase participation, but it is not sufficient. The creation of more free time for union members makes union participation possible, but it does not guarantee that extra time will be used for union activity rather than any other activity which individuals may prefer. Unions need to provide members with positive reasons for participation, and researchers need to investigate union participation in terms of motivators as well as obstacles.

The research findings suggest that the importance of work-related factors in explaining union participation applies for both women and men. Where workers are employed in jobs which promote awareness of social problems and which develop relevant skills for union work, such as the ability to negotiate and familiarity with how formal meetings are conducted, this can encourage union activism among both male and female workers. This confirms the findings of previous studies on trade unionism among social workers (Joyce, Corrigan and Hayes, 1988).

 When examining the relationship between women's work and their union participation, this study also illustrates the difficulties that some jobs presented for union activism. These jobs, such as nursery nurse, secretary and counter clerk, which were done predominantly by women, made union activism difficult chiefly because of the inflexibility of the work routines. These were also jobs which did not necessarily produce the social awareness or skills which promoted union activism. In these jobs it was frequently not possible to leave the job instantly to attend a union meeting or to see a member, even though the union facilities agreement permitted shop stewards to take as much time as reasonably necessary for union work. The significance of these job-related constraints on union activism suggests that part of the explanation for women's under-representation in union office-holding lies in occupational factors. In Feldberg and Glenn's (1979) terminology it is the job model rather than the gender model which needs to be considered first. Moreover, posts at more senior levels in local government, such as those at Senior Officer and Principal Officer grade, allowed the employee more autonomy in the work situation and therefore made union activism easier because work could be deferred and rescheduled to fit in with union activities. Far more male than female shop stewards were employed on these higher grades. The point at which gender factors came into operation was that women were more likely to express feelings of guilt than men were about leaving their job to do union work. This experience of guilt needs to be explained both in terms of socialization into the feminine gender role and also their typically lower occupational status.

The significance of work-related factors in influencing levels of union activism can also be seen in the operation of union facilities agreements. The research showed that male shop stewards did more of their union work in work time than female shop stewards did. This meant that the union facilities agreements were working better for male shop stewards, chiefly because of the greater flexibility of their jobs. Several interviewees commented on the need for cover for union work to make it feasible for workers in some jobs, such as typist and social worker, to take the facility time they were entitled to. The awareness of this issue, and particularly the linking of the problems of cover and under-representation of women in union office-holding, is evidence of the progress that was made in raising consciousness of equality issues in trade unions in the 1980s.

Towards the end of the research project, proposals for the merger of NALGO with COHSE and NUPE to form UNISON were being developed at national union level. UNISON was formed in July 1993 as a union with a predominantly female membership and with equality issues as a major part of the union agenda (Coote, 1992). NALGO's contribution to this agenda was well developed equality policies and a tradition of lay officers being involved in negotiations, which had produced a cadre of experienced women union activists. The discussion of where equality issues fit into a union's overall agenda raises the problem of similarities and differences in men's and women's trade union involvement, bargaining priorities and union cultures. Before unions move to adopt different bargaining priorities and styles of organizing in order to recruit and involve more female members, the issue should be explored of whether and to what extent women and men do have different priorities for union work. Trade unions in responding to the challenge of feminism and in recognizing the diversity of their membership have to find a balance between work on issues which involve all members and attention to sectional interests within unions. This research project found very little difference in bargaining priorities between male and female shop stewards. For both sexes the issue of higher pay for low-paid workers was the principal bargaining priority, an issue which covered both class and gender concerns. Where differences were identified with respect to collective bargaining, these lay not in bargaining priorities, but in styles of bargaining. Thus as a tentative conclusion to an on-going debate among industrial relations theorists about gender differences in collective bargaining, I would suggest that the gender differences may lie more in styles of bargaining than in bargaining priorities.

This difference in styles of bargaining relates to the issue of gender differences in union cultures. Writers such as Milkman (1985), Feldberg (1987), Cockburn (1991) and Faue (1991) have suggested that women have a different union culture from that of men and respond to different union organizing strategies. In this research study, this was clearly the case in respect of the meetings held in the nursery nurses' regrading campaign. In considering the relationship between union culture and women's level of union participation, it is important to keep in mind the possible importance of occupational status divisions among women. There is a need to investigate whether women at all levels in the occupational structure find traditional union cultures alienating and prefer alternative ways of organizing. It appeared from the interviews conducted in the research that women in professional jobs may be more comfortable than other women with participating in formal union meetings, because their work experience has to some degree emancipated them from the traditional feminine gender role and has equipped them with the requisite social skills. Thus gender differences in preferred styles of union organizing may be a more significant issue for women lower down the occupational structure.

Variations in support for female union activism, as indeed in general acceptance of equality issues, were found in different departmental cultures. While local government culture in general, compared with the culture of private sector businesses, may be supportive of women's equality (Cockburn, 1991), there were also noticeable variations within council departments. In those departments where more women were in senior jobs and there was a more radical culture, such as F&CS and Housing, it was easier for women to be openly feminist, without encountering social ostracism. This situation enabled women to be more assertive in various aspects of their working lives, including union activism.

The research indicates that the departmental factor in union activism is important and merits further study. For many shop stewards in this study the departmental level was the significant level of union activism. It was in the departmental shop stewards' committees, when they functioned well, that day-to-day problems of representing members were discussed and where much informal union training occurred. Where departmental shop stewards' committees were operating effectively they provided important support for union activists and probably did much to contribute to the survival of trade unionism in a difficult climate. In this study it appeared that trade unionism in local government had not merely survived through the 1980s, but had also achieved some worthwhile successes, such as regradings for groups of workers and a new technology agreement. In 1989 NALGO had held its first national strike, which had contributed to the defence of national conditions of service. Moreover branch life, and to an even greater extent union life at departmental level, was in some areas lively and vigorous, with frequent political debates among members and the periodic recruitment of new union office-holders.

Two clear factors which promote women's participation and representation in trade unions stand out from the research. The first factor is affirmative action in employment, so that as more women move into higher-status jobs, which give more flexibility in organizing work time, it becomes easier for them to encounter chief executives and senior managers on an equal basis in negotiations. This is important in terms of the job-related factors affecting union activism; higher occupational status may also diminish gender-role-related obstacles to union activism, since higher income allows women more financial independence and choice of lifestyle, and employment at more senior levels may promote self-confidence and social skills useful for union activism.

The second factor is the importance of trade union facilities agreements. The possible role of union facilities agreements in promoting female representation in unions was identified in the study of NUPE by Fryer *et al.* (1978). Informants repeatedly commented on the problem of the lack of cover for jobs which would have made it possible to take facility time. Obviously cover for shop stewards when doing union work is not likely to be provided while local government faces severe financial problems in raising sufficient revenue to provide services and to meet existing financial obligations. Many informants recognized this difficulty, but still saw the provision of cover as a long-term union objective. For some workers in some jobs, such as secretary and counter clerk, which are jobs disproportionately performed by women, cover is essential. Clearly this is an issue which should be high on the trade union bargaining agenda if economic circumstances improve. Often it is difficult for union activists to prioritize better facilities agreements in collective bargaining, because of a moralistic service ethic in voluntary organizations and the feeling that this is being selfish in prioritizing a claim which chiefly concerns union office-holders rather than the membership as a whole. Nonetheless, for unions to function as collective organizations and to be in a position to benefit their members, facility time, with cover where necessary, is important and should be prioritized more in collective bargaining. This is important for unions as an issue of both union democracy and equal opportunities, since it relates to both the right of the members to elect whoever they wish and the right of all members to stand for office, irrespective of occupation and gender.

There has been a surprising absence of research on women trade unionists given the growth of feminist research in many areas in recent years and the substantial gains that women have made within trade unions. Trade unions are a major part of the voluntary sector of organizations, and literature on equal opportunities (Cockburn, 1991) is beginning to show a recognition of the importance of equality in the voluntary sector for equality in employment generally. Thus study of women's position in trade unions should include recognition of the way progress towards greater equality in employment and in trade unions can be mutually supporting. The research reported in this study possesses the usual strengths and limitations of a field study of one union, which has concentrated on union office-holders. There is a case for further studies of gender and trade unions, and in different employment sectors. It is hoped that this book will encourage other researchers to conduct further studies of gender and trade unions. Such research may investigate matters such as gender and trade union bargaining priorities; the operation of trade union facilities agreements; gender and workplace/union cultures; and the departmental level of union organization. Moreover, if more organizations develop equal opportunities policies and take the responsibility of being an equal opportunity employer seriously, then there is the issue of how far affirmative action strategies in employment promote greater equality for women in trade unions and vice versa.

Bibliography

ABICHT, M. (1976) *Women's Leadership Roles in Two Selected Labour Unions in the United States and Belgium: A Comparative Descriptive Study*, DEd thesis, University of Cincinnatti.

AITKENHEAD, M. and LIFF, S. (1991) 'The Effectiveness of Equal Opportunity Policies', in FIRTH-COZENS, J. and WEST, M.A. (Eds) *Women at Work: Psychological and Organizational Perspectives*, Milton Keynes, Open University Press, pp. 26–41.

ANDERSON, J.C. (1979) 'Local Union Participation: A Re-Examination', *Industrial Relations*, Vol. 18, No. 1, pp. 18–31.

AYLAND, A.A. (1980) *Shop Stewards for NALGO? A Case Study of Four Branches*, University of Warwick MA thesis in Industrial Relations.

BADEN, N. (1986) 'Developing an Agenda: Expanding the Role of Women in Unions', *Labor Studies Journal*, Vol. 10, No. 3, pp. 229–49.

BANKING, INSURANCE AND FINANCE UNION (n.d.) [1982] *Equality for Women — Proposals for Positive Action*, BIFU.

BARRETT, M. and MCINTOSH, M. (1980) 'The "Family Wage": Some Problems for Socialists and Feminists', *Capital and Class*, No. 11, pp. 51–72.

BATSTONE, E., BORASTON, I. and FRENKEL, S. (1977) *Shop Stewards in Action: The Organization of Workplace Conflict and Accommodation*, Oxford, Basil Blackwell.

BAXANDALL, R. (1976) 'Women in American Trade Unions', in MITCHELL, J. and OAKLEY, A. (Eds) *The Rights and Wrongs of Women*, Harmondsworth, Penguin.

BEALE, J. (1982) *Getting it Together: Women as Trade Unionists*, London, Pluto.

BELL, D.E. (1985) 'Unionized Women in State and Local Government', in MILKMAN, R. (Ed.) *Women, Work and Protest*, London, Routledge and Kegan Paul, pp. 280–99.

BERGQUIST, V.A. (1974) 'Women's Participation in Labor Organizations', *Monthly Labor Review*, Vol. 97, No. 10, pp. 3–9.

BEYNON, H. and BLACKBURN, R.M. (1972) *Perceptions of Work: Variations within a Factory*, Cambridge, Cambridge University Press.

BLYTON, P.R. (1980) *Organizing Heterogeneous Employees within a White-Collar Union: A Study of Local Union Behaviour and Union-Management Relations*, PhD thesis, Sheffield University.

BLYTON, P. and URSELL, G. (1982) 'Vertical Recruitment in White-Collar Trade Unions: Some Causes and Consequences', *British Journal of Industrial Relations*, Vol. 20, No. 2, pp. 186–94.

BLYTON, P., NICHOLSON, N. and URSELL, G. (1981) 'Job Status and White-Collar Members' Union Activity', *Journal of Occupational Psychology*, Vol. 54, pp. 33–45.

BOSTON, S. (1987) *Women Workers and the Trade Unions*, London, Lawrence and Wishart.

BRACKX, A. (1977) 'Working for the Union', *Spare Rib*, No. 59, pp. 12–18.

BREITENBACH, E. (1981) 'A Comparative Study of the Women's Trade Union Conference and the Scottish Women's Trade Union Conference', *Feminist Review*, No. 7, pp. 65–86.

BRISKIN, L. and YANZ, L. (Eds) (1983) *Union Sisters: Women in the Labour Movement*, Toronto, Women's Educational Press.

BUCHANAN, R.T. (1985) 'Mergers in British Trade Unions 1949–1979', in MCCARTHY, W.E.J. (Ed.) *Trade Unions*, 2nd ed., Harmondsworth, Penguin, pp. 138–56.

BURTON, J.K. (1987) 'Dilemmas of Organizing Women Office Workers', *Gender and Society*, Vol. 1, No. 4, pp. 432–46.

CANTOR, M. and LAURIE, B. (Eds) (1977) *Class, Sex and the Woman Worker*, Westport, Connecticut, Greenwood Press.

CHARLES, N. (1983) 'Women and Trade Unions in the Workplace', *Feminist Review*, No. 15, pp. 3–22.

CHARLES, N. (1993) *Gender Divisions and Social Change*, Hemel Hempstead, Harvester Wheatsheaf.

COBBLE, D.S. (1990) 'Rethinking Troubled Relations between Women and Unions: Craft Unionism and Female Activism', *Feminist Studies*, Vol. 16, No. 3, pp. 519–48.

COCKBURN, C. (1983) *Brothers: Male Dominance and Technological Change*, London, Pluto.

COCKBURN, C. (1984) 'Trade Unions and the Radicalizing of Socialist Feminism', *Feminist Review*, No. 16, pp. 43–73.

COCKBURN, C. (1987) *Women, Trade Unions and Political Parties*, Fabian Research Series No. 349, London, Fabian Society.

COCKBURN, C. (1989) 'Equal Opportunities: the Short and Long Agenda', *Industrial Relations Journal*, Vol. 20, No. 3, pp. 213–25.

COCKBURN, C. (1991) *In the Way of Women: Men's Resistance to Sex Equality in Organizations*, London, Macmillan.

COLLING, T. and DICKENS, L. (1989) *Equality Bargaining — Why Not?*, London, Equal Opportunities Commission.

COOK, A.H. (1968) 'Women and American Trade Unions', *Annals of the American Academy of Political Science*, Vol. 375, pp. 124–33.

COOK, A.H., LORWIN, V.R. and DANIELS, A.K. (Eds) (1984) *Women and Trade Unions in Eleven Industrialized Countries*, Philadelphia, Temple University Press.

COOTE, A. (1992) 'Push Comes to Shove for the Sisters', *Observer*, 19 January.

COOTE, A. and KELLNER, P. (1980) *Hear This, Brother: Women Workers and Union Power*, London, New Statesman Report 1.

CROMPTON, R. and JONES, G. (1984) *White Collar Proletariat: Deskilling and Gender in Clerical Work*, London, Macmillan.

CUNNISON, S. (1983) 'Participation in Local Union Organization: School Meals Staff: A Case Study', in GAMARNIKOW, E., MORGAN, D., PURVIS, J. and TAYLORSON, D. (Eds) *Gender, Class and Work*, London, Heinemann, pp. 77–95.

DAVIS, E. (1981) 'Participation in Six Australian Trade Unions', *Journal of Industrial Relations*, Vol. 23, No. 2, pp. 190–215.

DEAN, L.R. (1954) 'Social Integration, Attitudes and Union Activity', *Industrial and Labor Relations Review*, Vol. 8, No. 1, pp. 48–58.

DELPHY, C. (1984) *Close to Home: A Materialist Analysis of Women's Oppression*, London, Hutchinson.

DEWEY, L.M. (1971) 'Women in Labour Unions', *Monthly Labour Review*, Vol. 94, pp. 42–8.

DICKENS, L., TOWNLEY, B. and WINCHESTER, D. (1984) *Tackling Sex Discrimination through Collective Bargaining: The Impact of Section 6 of the Sex Discrimination Act 1986*, London, Equal Opportunities Commission.

DOWNING, J. (1984) *Radical Media*, Boston, South End Press.

DUBIN, R. (1973) 'Attachment to Work and Union Militancy', *Industrial Relations*, Vol. 2, No. 1, pp. 51–64.

ELLIS, V. (1981) *The Role of Trade Unions in the Promotion of Equal Opportunities*, EOC/SSRC.

ELLIS, V. (1988) 'Current Trade Union Attempts to Remove Occupational Segregation in the Employment of Women', in WALBY, S. (Ed.) *Gender Segregation at Work*, Milton Keynes, Open University Press, pp. 135–56.

FAUE, E. (1991) *Community of Suffering and Struggle: Women, Men*

and the Labor Movement in Minneapolis 1915–1945, Chapel Hill
and London, University of North Carolina Press.

FELDBERG, R. (1987) 'Women and Trade Unions: Are We Asking the
Right Questions?', in BOSE, C., FELDBERG, R. and SOKOLOFF, N.
(Eds) *Hidden Aspects of Women's Work*, New York, Praeger, pp.
299–322.

FELDBERG, R.L. and GLENN, E.N. (1979) 'Male and Female: Job versus
Gender Models in the Sociology of Work', *Social Problems*, Vol.
26, No. 5, pp. 524–38.

FONOW, M.M. (1977) *Women in Steel: A Case Study of the Participation of Women in a Trade Union*, PhD thesis, Ohio State University.

FORM, W.H. and DANSERAU, H.K. (1957) 'Union Members' Orientations
and Patterns of Social Integration', *Industrial and Labor Relations Review*, Vol. 2, No. 1, pp. 3–12.

FOSH, P. (1981) *The Active Trade Unionist*, Cambridge, Cambridge
University Press.

FRIEDMAN, H. and MEREDEEN, S. (1980) *The Dynamics of Industrial
Conflict: Lessons from Ford*, London, Croom Helm.

FRYER, R.H., FAIRCLOUGH, A.J. and MANSON, T.B. (1978) 'Facilities for
Female Shop Stewards: The Employment Protection Act and
Collective Agreements', *British Journal of Industrial Relations*, Vol.
14, No. 2, pp. 160–74.

GENERAL AND MUNICIPAL WORKERS' UNION (1976) *Equality at Work —
The Way Forward*, London, GMWU.

GERMAN, L. (1989) *Sex, Class and Socialism*, London, Bookmarks.

GOLDMANN, H. (1974) *Emma Paterson*, London, Lawrence and Wishart.

GREEN, E., HEBRON, S. and WOODWARD, D. (1990) *Women's Leisure,
What Leisure?*, London, Macmillan.

GRIFFIN, G. (1981) 'Personal Characteristics and Industrial Militancy
in White-Collar Unions', *Journal of Industrial Relations*, Vol. 23,
No. 2, pp. 274–81.

HAMILTON, R. and BARRETT, M. (Eds) (1987) *The Politics of Diversity*,
London, Verso.

HANSARD SOCIETY (1990) *Women at the Top: Report of the Hansard
Society Commission*, London, Hansard Society.

HARDMAN, J. (1984) *Women in the Union*, PhD thesis, University of
Warwick.

HARRISON, M. (1979) 'Participation of Women in Trade Union
Activities: Some Research Findings and Comments', *Industrial
Relations Journal*, Vol. 10, No. 2, pp. 41–55.

HARTMANN, H. (1979) 'Capitalism, Patriarchy and Job Segregation by

Sex', In EISENSTEIN, Z.R. (Ed.) *Capitalist Patriarchy and the Case for Socialist Feminism*, New York, Monthly Review Press, pp. 206–47.

HEERY, E. and KELLY, J. (1988a) *Union Women: A Study of Women Trade Union Officers*, London, LSE.

HEERY, E. and KELLY, J. (1988b) 'Do Female Representatives Make a Difference? Women Full-Time Officials and Trade Union Work', *Work, Employment and Society*, Vol. 2, No. 4, pp. 487–505.

HEERY, E. and KELLY, J. (1989) ' "A Cracking Job for a Woman" — A Profile of Women Trade Union Officers', *Industrial Relations Journal*, Vol. 20, No. 3, pp. 192–202.

HERITAGE, J.C. (1977) *The Growth of Trade Unionism in the London Clearing Banks 1960–1970: A Sociological Interpretation*, PhD thesis, Leeds University.

HERITAGE, J. (1983) 'Feminisation and Unionisation: A Case Study from Banking', in GAMARNIKOW, E., MORGAN, D., PURVIS, J. and TAYLORSON, D. (Eds) *Gender, Class and Work*, London, Heinemann, pp. 131–48.

HUNT, J. (1982) 'A Woman's Place is in Her Union', in WEST, J. (Ed.) *Work, Women and the Labour Market*, London, Routledge and Kegan Paul, pp. 154–71.

HUNT, J. and ADAMS, S. (1980) *Women, Work and Trade Union Organization*, Workers' Educational Association.

INTERNATIONAL CONFEDERATION OF FREE TRADE UNIONS (1978) *Equality for Women in Trade Unions: A Programme of Action for the Integration of Women into Trade Union Organizations*, ICFTU.

IZRAELI, D.N. (1984) 'The Attitudinal Effects of Gender Mix in Union Committees', *Industrial and Labour Relations Review*, Vol. 37, No. 2, pp. 212–21.

JEWSON, N. and MASON, D. (1986) 'The Theory and Practice of Equal Opportunities Policies: Liberal and Radical Approaches, *Sociological Review*, Vol. 34, No. 2, pp. 307–34.

JOYCE, P., CORRIGAN, P. and HAYES, M. (1988) *Striking Out: Trade Unionism in Social Work*, London, Macmillan.

KANTER, R.M. (1977) *Men and Women of the Corporation*, New York, Basic Books.

KREBS, E. (1975) 'Women Workers and the Trade Unions in Austria', *International Labour Review*, Vol. 112, No. 4, pp. 265–78.

LABOUR RESEARCH DEPARTMENT (1988a) *Stress at Work*, London, Labour Research Department.

LABOUR RESEARCH DEPARTMENT (1988b) *Positive Action Guide: Bargaining for Equality*, London, Labour Research Department.

Bibliography

LABOUR RESEARCH DEPARTMENT (1989) *Winning Equal Pay: The LRD Guide to Job Evaluation and Equal Value*, London, Labour Research Department.

LABOUR RESEARCH DEPARTMENT (1990a) 'Union Reserved Seats — Creating a Space for Women', *Labour Research*, Vol. 79, No. 3, pp. 7–8.

LABOUR RESEARCH DEPARTMENT (1990b) 'Europe's Union Women', *Labour Research*, Vol. 79, No. 3, pp. 9–11.

LABOUR RESEARCH DEPARTMENT (1991) *Women in Trade Unions: Action for Equality*, London, Labour Research Department.

LABOUR RESEARCH DEPARTMENT (1992a) 'Challenging the Men in Suits', *Labour Research*, Vol. 81, No. 3, pp. 7–9.

LABOUR RESEARCH DEPARTMENT (1992b) 'Slow Progress in Euro-Unions', *Labour Research*, Vol. 81, No. 3, pp. 11–12.

LABOUR RESEARCH DEPARTMENT (1993) *Women, the Law and the Workplace*, London, Labour Research Department.

LAWRENCE, E. (1977) 'The Working Women's Charter Campaign', in MAYO, M. (Ed.) *Women in the Community*, London, Routledge and Kegan Paul, pp. 12–24.

LAWRENCE, E. (1992) *Shop Stewards in Local Government: The Influence of Occupation, Gender and Department on Union Activism*, PhD thesis, CNAA.

LEDGERWOOD, D.E. (1980) *An Analysis of the Satisfaction/Dissatisfaction of United States Female Unionists with their Local Trade Union Organizations: A View of the Coalition of Labor Union Women*, PhD thesis, University of Oklahoma.

LEDWITH, S., COLGAN, F., JOYCE, P. and HAYES, M. (1990) 'The making of Women Trade Union Leaders', *Industrial Relations Journal*, Vol. 21, No. 2, pp. 112–25.

LEMAN, P. (1980) *Organizing Women Workers: The Campaigns for Women's Rights in Three Trade Unions*, MA thesis, University of Warwick.

LEWENHAK, S.T. (1971) *Trade Union Membership among Women and Girls in the U.K. 1920–1965*, PhD thesis, LSE.

LEWENHAK, S. (1977) *Women and Trade Unions*, London, Ernest Benn.

LINN, I. (1977) *Shop Stewards in NALGO*, University of Warwick MA dissertation.

LIPSET, S.M., TROW, M. and COLEMAN, J. (1956) *Union Democracy: The Inside Politics of the International Typographical Union*, Glencoe, Free Press.

LOCKWOOD, D. (1958) *The Blackcoated Worker*, London, George Allen and Unwin.

LORWIN, V.L. (1979) 'Trade Unions and Women: The Most Difficult Revolution', in BROWN, B.E. (Ed.) *Eurocommunism and Euro-socialism: The Left Confronts Modernity*, Manchester, New Hampshire, Irvington, pp. 339–70.

LUMLEY, R. (1973) *White Collar Unionism in Britain*, London, Methuen.

MCCARTHY, M. (1977) 'Women in Trade Unions Today', in MIDDLETON, L. (Ed.) *Women in the Labour Movement*, London, Croom Helm, pp. 161–74.

MCILROY, J. (1988) *Trade Unions in Britain Today*, Manchester, Manchester University Press.

MARTIN, J. and ROBERTS, C. (1984) *Women and Employment: A Lifetime Perspective*, Department of Employment and Office of Population Censuses and Surveys, London, HMSO.

MAYBIN, R. (1980) 'NALGO, The New Unionism of Contemporary Britain', *Marxism Today*, Vol. 24, No. 1, pp. 17–21.

MILKMAN, R. (1985) 'Women Workers, Feminism and the Labor Movement since the 1960s', in MILKMAN, R. (Ed.) *Women, Work and Protest*, London, Routledge and Kegan Paul, pp. 300–22.

MOORE, R.J. (1980) 'The Motivation to Become a Shop Steward', *British Journal of Industrial Relations*, Vol. 18, No. 1, pp. 91–8.

NALGO (1975) *Equal Rights Working Party*, NALGO.

NALGO (1980) *NALGO Equal Rights Survey*, NALGO.

NALGO (1984) *How Equal are Your Opportunities?: Comparisons of Local Improvements Won by NALGO Branches*, NALGO.

NALGO (1988) 'Positive Action in NALGO: A Way Forward!', *NALGO News*, 25 November.

NALGO (n.d.) (a) *Campaigning for a Woman's Right to Choose*, NALGO.

NALGO (n.d.) (b) *Equal Opportunities: NALGO's Guide to Positive Action in Local Government*, NALGO.

NALGO (n.d.) (c) *Equality: It's about the Right to Make Choices*, NALGO.

NALGO (n.d.) (d) *51% Make It Count! A NALGO Guide to How Women Can Play a More Effective Part in the Union*, NALGO.

NALGO (n.d.) (e) *Getting our Members out of the Low Pay Ghetto*, NALGO.

NALGO (n.d.) (f) *Sex Discrimination in Pension Schemes*, NALGO.

NALGO (n.d.) (g) *Sexual Harassment is a Trade Union Issue*, NALGO.

NALGO (n.d.) (h) *Watch Your Language! Non-Sexist Language: A Guide for NALGO Members*, NALGO.

NALGO (n.d.) (j) *Workplace Nurseries: A Negotiating Kit*, NALGO.

NALGO AND THE EUROPEAN NETWORK OF WOMEN (n.d.) *Making the EEC work for Women*, NALGO.

NELSON, A. (1990) 'Equal Opportunities: Dilemmas, Contradictions, White Men and Class', *Critical Social Policy*, No. 28, pp. 25–42.

NEWMAN, G. (1982) *Path to Maturity: NALGO 1965–1980*, London, Cooperative Press Ltd.

NICHOLSON, N. (1976) 'The Role of the Shop Steward: An Empirical Case Study', *Industrial Relations Journal*, Vol. 7, pp. 15–26.

NICHOLSON, N. and URSELL, G. (1977) 'The NALGO Activists', *New Society*, 15 December, pp. 581–2.

NICHOLSON, N., URSELL, G. and BLYTON, P. (1981) *The Dynamics of White Collar Unionism*, London, Academic Press.

NUPE (n.d.) *Equal Value, Equal Pay: What it Means for Women in NUPE*, London, NUPE.

OAKLEY, A. (1972) *Sex, Gender and Society*, London, Temple Smith.

O'DONNELL, C. and HALL, P. (1988) *Getting Equal: Labour Market Regulation and Women's Work*, Sydney, Allen and Unwin.

PERLINE, M. and LORENZ, V. (1970) 'Factors Influencing Participation in Trade Union Activities', *American Journal of Economics and Society*, Vol. 29, pp. 425–37.

POOLE, M. (1974) 'Towards a Sociology of Shop Stewards', *Sociological Review*, Vol. 22, pp. 57–82.

PURCELL, K. (1979) 'Militancy and Acquiescence amongst Women Workers', in BURMAN, S. (Ed.) *Fit Work for Women*, London, Croom Helm, pp. 112–33.

RAMAZANOGLU, C. (1989) *Feminism and the Contradictions of Oppression*, London, Routledge.

REES, T. (1990) 'Gender, Power and Trade Union Democracy', in FOSH, P. and HEERY, E. (Eds) *Trade Unions and their Members*, Basingstoke, Macmillan, pp. 177–205.

REES, T. (1992) *Women and the Labour Market*, London, Routledge.

REES, T. and REED, M. (1981) *Equality? Report of a Survey of NALGO Members*, London, NALGO.

ROBY, R. and UTTAL, L. (1988) 'Trade Union Stewards: Handling Union, Family and Employment Responsibilities', in GUTEK, B.A., STROMBERG, A.H. and LARWOOD, L. (Eds) *Women and Work: An Annual Review*, Vol. 3, Newbury Park, California, Sage, pp. 215–48.

ROSE, M. (1985) *Reworking the Work Ethic*, London, Batsford.

SERTUC WOMEN'S COMMITTEE (n.d.) *Still Moving Towards Equality*, SERTUC [South East Regional Council of the TUC].

SOCIETY OF CIVIL AND PUBLIC SERVANTS (1982) *Equality the Next Step: The Changing Role of Women in the Civil Service*, SCPS.

SOLDON, N.C. (1978) *Women in British Trade Unions, 1874–1976*, Dublin, Gil! and Macmillan.

SOLDON, N.C. (Ed.) (1985) *The World of Women's Trade Unionism: Comparative Historical Essays*, Westport Connecticut, Greenwood Press.

SPINRAD, W. (1960) 'Correlates of Trade Union Participation: A Summary of the Literature', *American Sociological Review*, Vol. 25, pp. 237–44.

SPOOR, A. (1967) *White Collar Union: Sixty Years of NALGO*, London, Heinemann.

STAGEMAN, J. (1980) *Women in Trade Unions*, Occasional Paper No. 6, Hull, University of Hull, Department of Adult Education, Industrial Studies Unit.

STONE, I. (1984) *Positive Action Report*, Sheffield City Council Employment Department.

TANNENBAUM, A.S. and KAHN, R.L. (1958) *Participation in Union Locals*, Evanston, Illinois, Row, Peterson and Co.

TERRY, M. (1982) 'Organizing a Fragmented Workforce: Shop Stewards in Local Government', *British Journal of Industrial Relations*, Vol. 20, No. 1, pp. 1–19.

TILL-RETZ, R. (1986) 'Unions in Europe: Increasing Women's Participation', *Labor Studies Journal*, Vol. 10, No. 3, pp. 250–60.

TRADES UNION CONGRESS (1984) *Equality for Women within Trade Unions*, TUC.

TRADES UNION CONGRESS (1986) *Positive Action Programmes: a TUC Guide towards Equality of Opportunity for Women*, London, TUC.

TREBILCOCK, A. (1991) 'Strategies for Strengthening Women's Participation in Trade Union Leadership', *International Labour Review*, Vol. 130, No. 4, pp. 407–26.

UNDY, R., ELLIS, V., MCCARTHY, W.E.J. and HALMOS, A.M. (1985) 'Recent Merger Movements and Future Union Structure', in MCCARTHY, W.E.J. (Ed.) *Trade Unions*, 2nd ed., Harmondsworth, Penguin, pp. 157–68.

URSELL, G., NICHOLSON, N. and BLYTON, P. (1981) 'Processes of Decision Making in a Trade-Union Branch', *Organisation Studies*, Vol. 2, No 1, pp. 45–72.

WADDINGTON, J. (1988) 'Trade Union Mergers: A Study of Trade Union Structural Dynamics', *British Journal of Industrial Relations*, Vol. 24, No. 3, pp. 409–30.

Bibliography

WALTON, J. (1985) *A Woman's Place is in her Union — A Study of Women Shop Stewards in the Kent County Branch of NALGO*, University of Kent at Canterbury Women's Studies Occasional Papers, No. 5.

WEBB, J. and LIFF, S. (1988) 'Play the White Man: The Social Construction of Fairness and Competition in Equal Opportunity Policies', *Sociological Review*, Vol. 36, No. 3, pp. 532–51.

WEINSTEIN, J. (1986) 'Angry Arguments across the Picket Lines: Left Labour Councils and White Collar Trade Unionism', *Critical Social Policy*, No. 17, pp. 41–60.

WERTHEIMER, B.M. and NELSON, A.H. (1975) *Trade Union Women: A Study of their Participation in New York City Locals*, New York, Praeger.

Index

Abortion Act (1967) 29
abortion rights
  policies 23, 28–9
    NALGO 37
  support 142
activism *see* participation, women's
adjournment venues 32
affirmative action
  policies 29–30, 155
    support 140
  Sheffield 45–6
Alton Anti-Abortion Bill 29
Amalgamated Engineering Union
    (AEU)
  exclusion of women 2
  Sheffield Communist Party 44
Anti-Abortion Bills 28, 29
Anti-Apartheid Movement 37
Anti-Nazi League 37
assertiveness 111, 112, 113
  training 146, 147–9
Association of Cinematograph,
    Television and Allied
    Technicians (ACTT) 23
  equal pay 28
Association of Professional,
    Executive, Clerical, and
    Computer Staff (APEX) 45
Association of Scientific, Technical
    and Managerial Staffs (ASTMS)
  participation 16
  women members, increase in 30
attitudes
  to being a shop steward 99–102
  to work 90–1
average gross hourly earnings 3

babysitting expenses 31, 122
Baltimore Working Women Group
    24
banking industry 16–17
bargaining *see* collective bargaining
barriers to participation 6–7, 12–13,
    15–17
  overcoming 31–2
black women
  Sheffield council 45
  venues of meetings 32
Blain, Herbert 35
Blunkett, David 44
  rate-capping 50
boycotts of posts 35
branch committees
  occupational distribution 64
  union 'careers' 98
branch officers *see* office-holding
British Leyland 37
bureaucratization 36

career prospects
  gender inequalities 112–13, 143
  occupational structure 56
  in unions 97–9
  union participation 12, 17, 66–7
Case Con 36
chief shop stewards
  occupational distribution 63
  union facility agreements 74
child care assistants (CCAs) 59
  see also nursery nurses
children *see* family structure
childcare
  campaigns 33

at meetings 31, 122–3
  babysitting expenses 31, 122
nursery provision 140, 146–7
shop stewards 87–90, 113
Chile Solidarity Campaign 37
civil service 3, 27
clerical career grade 62–3
Coalition of Labor Union Women
  (CLUW)
  formation 33
  leadership 20
  structure 23–5, 26
collective bargaining
  gender differences 128–36, 153
  local and national 37, 39–40, 57
  priorities and occupation 69–70
  women's interests
    equal pay 27
    failure to represent 2
    positive action 30
commitment to work
  gender 90–1
  union participation 11–13, 16
committees
  branch
    occupational distribution
      64
    union 'careers' 98
    union 21–2
    women's rights 32–3
Communist Party, Sheffield 44
Confederation of Health Service
  Employees (COHSE) 1, 41–2,
  153
conferences, women delegates 4
confidence 96, 100
Co-operative Movement, Sheffield
  44
Corrie Anti-Abortion Bill 29
cover
  participation encouragement 123,
    155
  union facility agreements 72–6,
    80, 105–6, 109–10
creches 31, 122–3

culture
  departmental 154
    shop stewards 68–9, 92–4
  union 153–4
    women's interests 25

Data Preparation staff
  new technology dispute 49
  occupational segregation 54
democracy, union 19, 81
demonstrations, abortion rights
  29
Department of Employment and
  Economic Development 43
departmental representatives
  culture 68–9, 92–4, 154
  and shop stewards 47, 154
discrimination 111–13
District Labour Party (DLP) 45
diversity in trade union movement
  4–5
domestic responsibilities 31
domestic situation *see* family
  structure

Eastern Europe trade unions 1
economic independence 16
Education Department
  job grades 55
    regrading 59–60, 61
  national strike 39
  shop stewards
    departmental culture 92–3
    women's under-representation
    96–7
election of shop stewards 94–5
electricity industry 36
Employment Department
  industrial action 71
  job grades 55
employment patterns, Sheffield
  42–3
engineering industry 42, 43
equal opportunities
  legislation 140

NALGO
   campaigns 33
   commitment to 8
   policies 145–9
   non-representation of members
      137–8
   policy limitations 46
   positive action 30
   Sheffield City Council 45
   union role 2, 143–4
equal pay
   history 3
      in local government 57–8
   policies 27–8
Equal Pay Act (1970) 3, 27
   limitations 29
Equal Pay Amendment Act (1984)
   introduction 3
   limitations 29
Equal Rights Working Party
      Report (1975) 33
equal value 61
equity, pay 27
ethic, work 13
European Community
   participation encouragement 31
   women's rights policies 26
exclusion of women from unions 2, 3

facility agreements
   gender 91, 105–10, 152–3, 155
   and occupation 19, 72–80
   personal life 113–14
   shop steward turnover 81
Family and Community Services
      (F&CS) Department
   conflicts 48
      new technology 49
   job grades 55
      regrading 60
   shop stewards 47, 68
      departmental culture 92, 93, 94
family structure
   gender role and work role 5–6
   leaders, union 20–1

local government 58
low-income husbands 16
office-holding 20, 87–90, 118
participation, union 16, 18, 114
family wage 3, 27
feminine gender role 7
feminist perspectives, gender
      differences 85
feminist politics
   equal opportunities 146
   structure of unions 25, 26
   union leaders 20, 21
   union participation 17
flexibility, job
   representation of women 82
   union office-holding 72, 78–9
      gender 91–2, 109
Ford 3, 27, 28

gender roles 84–5
   departmental cultures 93
   oppression by 140
   and work roles 5–7
General and Municipal Workers'
      Union (GMWU) 19
General, Municipal and Boiler-
      makers' Union (GMB) 27
grades, job
   bargaining priorities 70
   gender 86
   industrial action 71–2
   local government 54, 55–7
   office-holding 63–4, 66–7
   regrading disputes 58–61
   Sheffield council 45
   union facility agreements 77,
      78–80
   union participation 16
gross hourly earnings 3

Hayward *v.* Cammell Laird 27
hierarchy, occupational 12
Hill, Levi 35
history
   of equal pay in local government
      57–8

of NALGO 35–8
  Sheffield 46–8
of women and unions 2–5
  research literature 14
Hotel Employees and Restaurant
    Employees' (HERE)
    International Union 18
Housing Benefits 51
Housing Department
  conflicts 48
    new technology 49
    poll tax 51
  shop stewards 68
    departmental culture 93
    women's under-representation
      97
husbands *see* family structure

independence, economic 16
industrial action 3
  and gender 103–5
  and occupation 70–2
  see also strikes
industrial tribunal applications 3
International Confederation of Free
    Trade Unions (ICFTU) 31
international relations
    sub-committee 48

job-sharing 132

Labour councils 37–8
Labour Group, Sheffield 44
  positive action 45
labour market, Sheffield 44
Labour Party 43, 44
Land and Planning Department
  national strike 40
  occupational structure 55–6
  regrading 60
language, non-sexist 32
late work 77
leadership skills
  developed by activism 2
  and waitressing skills 18

leaders, women as
  emergence 1
  research literature 14, 20–2
  reserved places 3, 33–4
  under-representation 4, 5, 14
Libraries Department
  gender inequalities 143
  job grades 55
Liverpool Municipal Officers' Guild
    35
local bargaining 37
local government
  equal pay 3
  occupational structure 54–63
  see also National and Local
    Government Officers'
    Association (NALGO)
London County Council 58
London Municipal Officers'
    Association 35
London Trades Council 28
low pay
  bargaining priorities 129, 130–1,
    132–3
  local government 62–3
lunch-hour meetings 32

Macarthur, Mary 1
Managerial, Administrative,
    Technical and Supervisory
    Association (MATSA) 45
managers
  harassment by 111–13
  pressure from 107
marital status *see* family structure
'masculine' behaviour 25
masculine gender role 7
maternal instinct 140
meetings, union
  attendance 16
  childcare responsibilities 31
  timing 16
    to encourage participation
      31–2, 123
  venues 16, 32

membership of unions
  continuous, and office-holding
    20
  NALGO 8, 37
  women, numbers 1, 2, 4, 8
    increase 30–1
  see also participation, women's;
    representation of women
mergers, union 41–2
  Unison 1, 41, 153
militancy 16
minimum wage 28
motivating factors for participation
  6–7, 11–13, 15

Nalgo Action Group 36, 47
National Abortion Campaign 29,
  37
National and Local Government
    Officers' Association
    (NALGO)
  abortion rights 29
  bargaining 128–9, 136
    priorities 130–1
  equal rights policies 145–9
  gender inequalities, awareness of
    140, 142
  grading system 56–7
  history 35–8, 46–8
  membership 30, 45
  National Equal Opportunities
    Committee 33
  new technology dispute 48–50,
    104
  non-sexist language 32
  office-holding, women's under-
    representation 19–20
  participation
    commitment to work 11–12
    promotion of women's 5, 34
  pay
    equal 28, 58
    low 62
  poll tax 50–2
  rate-capping 50

regrading disputes 58–61
representation of women
  occupation 82
  promotion 122–5
sexual harassment policy 136–8
Sheffield 7–8
shop stewards 100
strikes 36–41, 71, 104–5
union 'careers' 99
union leaders 20
Unison formation 1, 41–2, 153
women's interests 23
Working Women's Charter 28
National Association of Teachers in
    Further and Higher Education
    (NATFHE) 23
  equal pay 28
national bargaining 37, 39–40,
  57
National Equal Opportunities
    Committee 33
national executive committees 4
National Federation of Women
    Workers 1
national minimum wage 28
National Organization of Working
    Women: 9 to 5
  formation 33
  structure 23–6
national salary scales 35, 36, 56–7
national strike (NALGO, 1989)
  38–41, 71, 104–5
National Union of Public
    Employees (NUPE)
  national minimum wage 28
  shop stewards 47
    part-time women workers 6
    under-representation of women
      19
  Unison formation 1, 41–2, 153
nursery nurses
  feminine gender role 7
  regrading 59–60, 61, 95–6
    industrial action 103–4
nursery provision 140, 146–7

occupational communities 18
occupational differences 6
occupational segregation
  changes 23
  local government 54–5
  union participation 16–17, 18
occupational structure 54–63
office-holding
  attitudes 64–9, 90–1, 99–102
  bargaining priorities 69–70
  childcare 87–90
  departmental cultures 92–4
  election 94–5
  equal opportunities training 145
  gender 84–7, 116–21
  industrial action 103–5
  inequality, awareness of 139–45
  job status 91–2
  management harassment 111–13
  NALGO 122–5
    development 36
    Sheffield 7–8, 46–7
  numbers 4
  NUPE 47
  occupational distribution 63–4
  part-time workers 6
  and participation 11–13
  personal life 113–16
  positive action 30
  promotion 7, 80–1
  research literature 19–20
  turnover 80–1, 110–11
  under-representation of women
    95–7
  union careers 97–9
  union facility agreements 72–4,
    75–80, 105–10

paid employment, women's role 2–3
part-time workers
  office-holding 6
    under-representation 19
  as shop stewards 6
participation, women's
  encouraging 31, 33–4

feminine gender role 7
history 2–5
influencing factors 6–7, 11–13,
  15–17, 31–2, 151–6
leadership skills 2
  and office-holding 11–13
research literature 14–18
women's rights policies 26
worker unity 4
see also membership of unions;
  representation of women
passive woman worker thesis 16
Paterson, Emma 1
patriarchy perspective, gender
  differences 85
pay 69–70
  equal
    history 3, 57–8
    policies 27–8
  low
    bargaining priorities 129,
      130–1, 132–3
    local government 62–3
  performance-related 58
personal lives 113–16
policies, union 22–6
political parties 17
poll tax 50–2
positive action
  policies 29–30, 155
    support 140
  Sheffield 45–6
Positive Action Report 45–6
  occupational segregation 54
  occupational structure 55, 56
prejudice, male 15
pregnant women, and VDUs 50
pressures of work 76–7
printworkers 18
promotion
  prospects
    gender inequalities 112–13, 143
    occupational structure 45
    union participation 12, 17, 66–7
  shop steward turnover 7, 80–1

public expenditure 37–8
public life, unions as route to 2

qualifications 54–5
quota systems 33–4

racial harassment 32, 137
radicalization 36–7
rate-capping
  NALGO 38
  Sheffield 44, 50
regrading disputes 58–61
relevance of trade unions 1–2
reluctant shop stewards 65
representation of women 30–4
  encouraging 33–4
  history 2–5
  occupation 82
  Sheffield NALGO 7–8
  see also membership of unions;
    participation, women's
reserved places 3, 33–4
Roe *v.* Wade 29
role models 93, 120–1

salary levels 54
  see also pay
Saturday working 17
school meals staff
  regrading 61
  union structure 23
segregation, occupational
  changes 23
  local government 54–5
  union participation 16–17, 18
self-criticism 102
service conditions 69–70, 130–1
Service Employees' International
    Union (SEIU) 24–5, 26
Sex Discrimination Act (1975) 29
Sex Discrimination Amendment
    Act (1986) 29
sexism 31
  overcoming 32

sexual harassment
  bargaining priorities 131, 133
  union policy 136–9
Sheffield
  employment patterns 42–3
  labour movement 44
  Trades Council 44
Sheffield City Council
  employment patterns 43, 44
  new technology dispute 48–9
  positive action 45
  rate-capping 50
shop stewards *see* office-holding
single-sex unionism 2, 3
single status proposals 48
skewed groups 22
skills
  bargaining 134–5
  leadership
    developed by activism 2
    and waitressing skills 18
Social Charter 26
social workers
  NALGO strike action 36
  union participation 13
socialist feminists 85–6
society, gender roles in 5, 6
Society of Graphical and Allied
    Trades (SOGAT) 20
solidarity in union movement
    4
Soviet Union, former 1
sponsorship 21
status, job
  gender 91–2
  union participation 12, 16
steel industry
  Sheffield 42, 43
  union participation 16
stress
  of union activism 113–16
  of work 68, 113
strikes
  for equal pay 3, 27, 28
  and gender 103–5

NALGO 36-7
  national (1989) 38-41, 71,
    104-5
  new technology 49
  nursery nurses 59, 103-4
  and occupation 71
structure
  of meetings 123-4
  occupational 54-63
  union
    participation 18
    responsiveness to women's
      interests 22-6
support for office-holders
  new stewards 94
  union work 79, 107-8, 114-17
  women 20

teaching 3, 27
technology, new
  bargaining priorities 131-2
  dispute 48-50, 104
textile unions 3
tilted groups 22
time conflicts 72-8, 80, 106-8
timing of meetings
  attendance 16
  to encourage women's
    participation 31-2, 123
token situation 22
toughness 25
trade boards 27
Trades Councils
  Sheffield 44
  Working Women's Charter 28
Trades Union Congress (TUC)
  abortion rights 28, 29
  equal pay resolution 3
  NALGO affiliation 36
  participation of women 31
  positive action 30
  Willis, Norman 1
  women delegates 4
  Working Women's Charter 28
training of shop stewards 94

Treasury Department
  departmental culture 93
  new technology dispute 49
  occupational segregation 54
  occupational structure 56
  poll tax 50-1
Trico-Folberth 3, 28
turnover, shop stewards
  and gender 110-11
  and occupation 80-1

under-representation of women 4,
  5
  research literature 14, 19-20
  views of 95-7
Union of Shop, Distributive and
    Allied Workers (USDAW)
    19
Union Women's Alliance to Gain
    Equality (Union WAGE) 24
Unison 1, 41-2, 153

venues of meetings
  attendance 16
  to encourage women's
    participation 32
visual display units (VDUs) 50

wages councils 27
waitresses 18
White Anti-Abortion Bill 28, 29
white-collar workers 12
Whitley Councils
  equal pay 58
  NALGO 36, 56
Willis, Norman 1
women-only unions 3
women's interests, union
    responsiveness to 14, 22-6
women's movement 17
women's rights
  advisory committees and
    conferences 3
  developing structures for 32-3
  NALGO 37